Preface

In his account of a journey through Wales with Baldwin, Archbishop of Canterbury, Gerald of Wales tells us that they called, in early April 1188, at the abbey of Strata Florida. They were welcomed as guests, and they stayed there for some time. Gerald says nothing about the abbey, its inhabitants or how they lived, because his readers would have been familiar with monasteries and how they worked. For most people today, even though Cistercian monasteries continue to exist, the lives of monks and lay brothers are wholly unfamiliar. It can be difficult, when visiting the ruins of the abbey buildings at Strata Florida, to imagine who the inhabitants were and how they spent their days.

This publication, the fourth in a series of short explanatory books on Strata Florida, is designed to make good this gap in understanding. It aims to summarise what we know about medieval Cistercian monks and their way of life: how they became monks, how their behaviour was governed by regulations, how they conducted their religious services and rituals, how they studied, worked, ate and slept. We learn, too, about the *conversi* or lay brothers, who carried out most of the manual tasks of the abbey, and about how visitors and guests were welcomed.

The Strata Florida Trust is very grateful to Janet Burton, Professor of Medieval History at the University of Wales Trinity St David, for preparing this guide. Janet is one of the leading authorities on the monastic foundations of Wales and she brings many years of research on the Cistercians to bear on her subject.

The Strata Florida Trust is a registered charity and has two aims: to restore the farm next to the Abbey, Mynachlog Fawr, and to use its buildings to create a Strata Florida Centre for people to learn about archaeology and conservation, Welsh culture and history, and the natural environment. We hope that you will enjoy reading *Life in a Medieval Cistercian Monastery*, that it will help enrich your experience of visiting this remarkable site, and that the work of the Trust will interest you.

Andrew Green
Chair, Strata Florida Trust

Life in a Medieval Cistercian Monastery

Since the third century after the birth of Christ, Christians might seek to worship God by withdrawing from the world and its concerns either to live alone or as a member of a community of like-minded people. This is the phenomenon we know as monasticism. Those who lived a solitary life were known as hermits or anchorites, and the earliest recorded lived in Egypt and Palestine. Those who lived in communities (monasteries) committed themselves to a common life, renouncing personal property, and to following a rule, that is, a set of written guidelines that laid out how they should spend their days and how their communities should be governed. The most famous and influential of these was the Rule of St Benedict, compiled by the sixth-century Italian abbot whose name it bears.

Fig. 1: The famous Coptic Christian monastery of St Simeon in Aswan, Egypt, dating from between the sixth and eighth centuries.

Strata Florida was one such community. Founded in 1164 and famously associated with Lord Rhys (Rhys ap Gruffudd), the leading ruler of south Wales in the second half of the twelfth century, it belonged to an international monastic movement known as the Cistercian Order. This took its name from the mother house, Cîteaux, which is located in the area of France known as Burgundy. This book seeks to describe life in a Cistercian monastery so that, as we walk around what remains of the abbey church and precinct in their broader landscape setting, we may imagine the life of a community that inhabited the site for nearly four hundred years until its dissolution in 1539.

Fig. 2:

The siting of Strata Florida on the western edge of the Cambrian Mountains in Ceredigion, Wales. This aerial view taken by Toby Driver of the Royal Commission on the Ancient and Historical Monuments of Wales (RCAHMWAP20074936) looks westwards across the valley of the Afon Teifi towards the Irish Sea in the far distance where stood the abbey grange and port of Aber-arth. The abbey precinct is shaded in red. Circled are the remains of the abbey's core buildings, centred today on the farm of Mynachlog Fawr. These former farm buildings are now owned by the Strata Florida Trust and are the focus of on-going research and archaeological excavation.

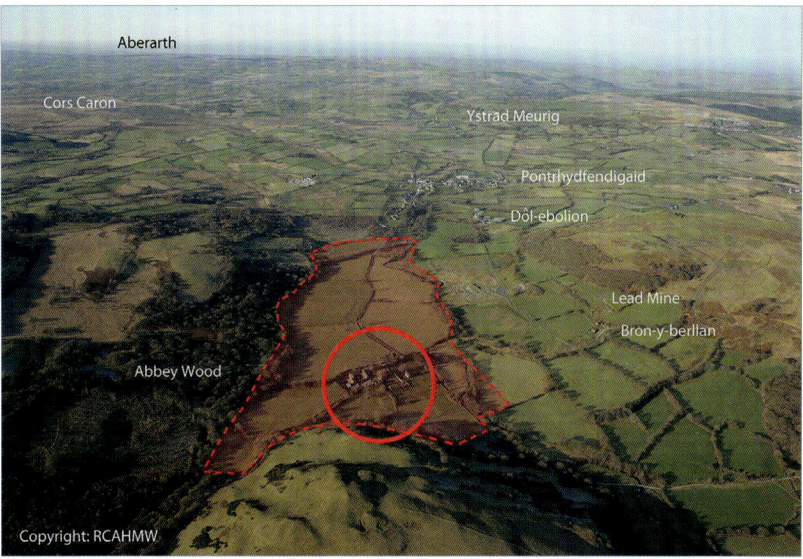

The following account is based partly on what we call 'normative texts', that is, documents produced by monastic legislators to lay down the basis of monastic practice. In the case of the Cistercian Order these documents were the Rule of St Benedict, which became the basis of monastic life in the West, and the Cistercian *Carta caritatis* (the 'Charter of Love'), first composed by Abbot Stephen Harding of Cîteaux (1109–1133/4). Stephen, an Englishman born in Dorset who, after a mixed career ended as a monk and then abbot of Cîteaux, intended the *Carta* to be a means of encouraging uniformity among houses of the Order. From time to time these were reinforced or supplemented by rules and regulations drawn up by the Cistercian General Chapter, an annual meeting of abbots held at Cîteaux. A word of caution should be sounded. Not all communities were able to follow all these guidelines all the time. Local circumstances – topography, pressures from founders and patrons, social organisation, economy, natural disaster, extreme weather conditions, warfare, conquest, and colonisation – all these determined that there might be variations in practice. This book seeks to balance accounts of daily life and routine as laid down by normative texts with evidence derived from other sources, such as chronicles, saints' lives, and *exempla* or short stories (usually with a moral purpose) from Cistercian writers. But first we should ask: who were the Cistercians?

How it all began ...

Our story begins in or shortly before 1098. In that year a group of monks from the Benedictine monastery of Molesme in the Côte d'Or region of France, led by their abbot, Robert, stood before a powerful churchman, Hugh, archbishop of Lyon. Hugh was also a papal legate, that is, he was a special delegate of the pope empowered to act as his representative. The monks' purpose was to express their dissatisfaction at the laxity of monastic observance at Molesme and in particular the failure to observe fully the Rule of St Benedict. As we have noted, this rule was the basis of monastic observance and the charge laid by the brothers of Molesme was therefore a serious one. Hugh was convinced by their arguments, and as a result allowed them to return briefly to Molesme before striking out to find another place where they could live in greater simplicity and poverty. Thus begins the account of the origins of the monastery of Cîteaux, known as the *Exordium parvum* (the 'Little Beginning'). The author was not named – though he was clearly a Cistercian monk – and he probably began to write in the 1120s, some two decades after the foundation of the monastery.

Cistercian narratives, such as the *Exordium parvum*, were from time to time rewritten, added to, and refashioned to suit new contexts. The main outlines of what happened in 1098 and the years to follow are clear enough, however, and the greatest and most successful experiment in medieval monastic history began with the departure of Robert and his monks for a site described as a wilderness, a 'desert', a place far from human habitation. There they cleared the ground, built a simple wooden monastery, and, with the permission of the local bishop, began monastic life under Robert, now abbot of what was at first known as the New Monastery.

Fig. 3: Cîteaux as depicted in an engraving of 1674 by Brissart before it was largely destroyed after the French Revolution. Key features include the compact body of major buildings including the church set around a cloister and all surrounded by a precinct wall within which are also gardens and orchards (Bibliothèque Nationale de France).

The foundation narratives, especially the *Exordium parvum*, were keen to stress that the new foundation enjoyed the protection and authority of the Church – the pope and a number of bishops. Moreover, they aligned the New Monastery with two important traditions. The use of words such as 'desert', 'wilderness', and 'solitude' was intended to recall the deserts of Egypt and Palestine, where, in the third century, monasticism had been born. There, the monastic life was solitary, lived by monks on their own or in small groups, away from the cities and centres of population of the Roman Empire. A second important feature of the *Exordium parvum* is the stress on the Rule of St Benedict, which Benedict himself called a 'little rule for beginners'. We will be returning to the Rule shortly to learn how Benedict envisaged daily life within his monastery. By 1098, when Robert and his monks left Molesme, monasticism still represented a life withdrawn from society for those individuals who chose it. However, as corporations, monasteries were often closely enmeshed in the broader communities in which they were located. They were powerful (and often rich) institutions to which the elite of society turned for prayers for their own salvation. Monasteries did not just serve the spiritual needs of those who entered their walls. They interceded for the wellbeing of humankind.

Tradition and Innovation

The Cistercians were, in one way, traditionalists. They appealed to the monastic past – the very roots of monasticism in the East – and to the Rule of St Benedict, the ultimate monastic authority in the West. In other ways they were innovators. Quite what was in the minds of the monks who left Molesme in 1098 we cannot know. What we can be sure of is that in the years that followed they developed into what has been described as the first monastic order, moving from an interpretation of the Latin word *ordo* meaning simply a way of life, to a usage denoting a congregation of houses held together by an ambitious administrative machinery. The stimulus for these developments was surely the beginning of the phenomenal spread of houses from the New Monastery, initially to the area around Cîteaux. In 1113 a group of monks left to establish a monastery at La Ferté (Saône-et-Loire). Pontigny (Yonne) followed in 1114, and in 1115 the most famous of all Cistercians, St Bernard, led a group to Clairvaux (Aube), there to be its abbot until his death in 1153. By 1118 the Cistercians were expanding into a third generation. Some abbeys were already in existence, and voluntarily joined the new order, accepting its customs. Others were newly founded (*de novo*).

Fig. 4:
The geography of Cistercian foundation and colonization from its Burgundian core into England, Wales, and Scotland, from the Cadw guidebook.

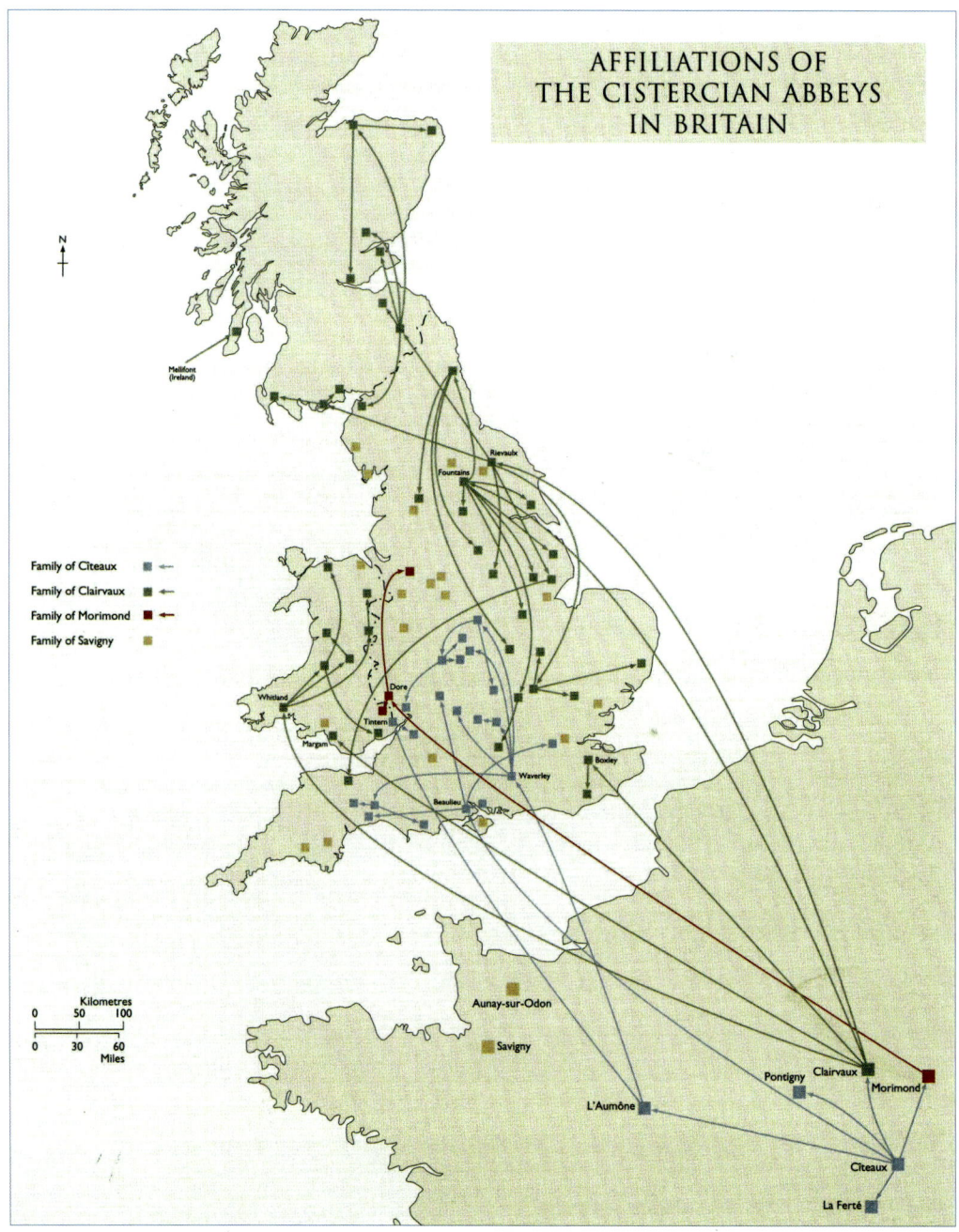

It was in this context of growth that Stephen Harding, the English-born abbot of Cîteaux, created the first version of a document known as the *Carta caritatis*, the 'Charter of Love'. This outlined how Cistercian houses were to sustain the bonds of love that underpinned their Order. Here we find the innovation. Each year, the abbot of each Cistercian house was to make the journey to Cîteaux for the General Chapter, which came to be held in September. There they discussed matters of interest to the Order, disciplined any wayward abbots, appointed some of their number to investigate disputes between houses, and – as and when it was deemed necessary – passed regulations intended to ensure adherence to the Rule of St Benedict and good monastic observance.

Fig. 5:
Manuscript of the *Carta caritatis*: image from Vorarlberger Nachrichten, December 2019.

Until fairly recently, Cistercian women have largely been ignored in scholarship on the Order. This is partly a reflection on the male-orientated nature of the official documentary evidence, which tends to assume only male participation. It is also related to an uneasiness on the part of historians as to how – if at all – women fitted into the familial structure of the Order and its bureaucratic machinery. It is now accepted that from the beginnings of Cîteaux, Cistercian men such as Stephen Harding and Abbot Bernard of Clairvaux (later canonised as St Bernard) encouraged female monastic vocation, and that Cistercian abbeys for women did exist, even if their way of life and constitution differed from male houses in some respects.

Fig. 6:
Women of the Cistercian Order (British Library, MS Yates Thompson 11, f. 1v, c. 1290) Note the key role of men in the conduct of the liturgy.

'Transplanted Across Many Seas…'

At a remarkably early date – within a quarter of a century of the foundation of Cîteaux – an English Benedictine monk named William of Malmesbury was able to write that the Cistercians were by then perceived to be 'the surest road to Heaven'. Was it their reputation for holiness, their simplicity and austerity, or their impressive organisation that appealed to founders and patrons who gave of their material resources to build Cistercian monasteries and sustain the life of the monks and women religious? The answer must surely be a combination of all these factors, and others. What is not in doubt is that for several decades, kings, princes, members of the nobility, archbishops, and bishops, founded Cistercian houses all over Europe and beyond.

Fig. 7:
Indication of the spread of Cistercian monasteries across Europe.

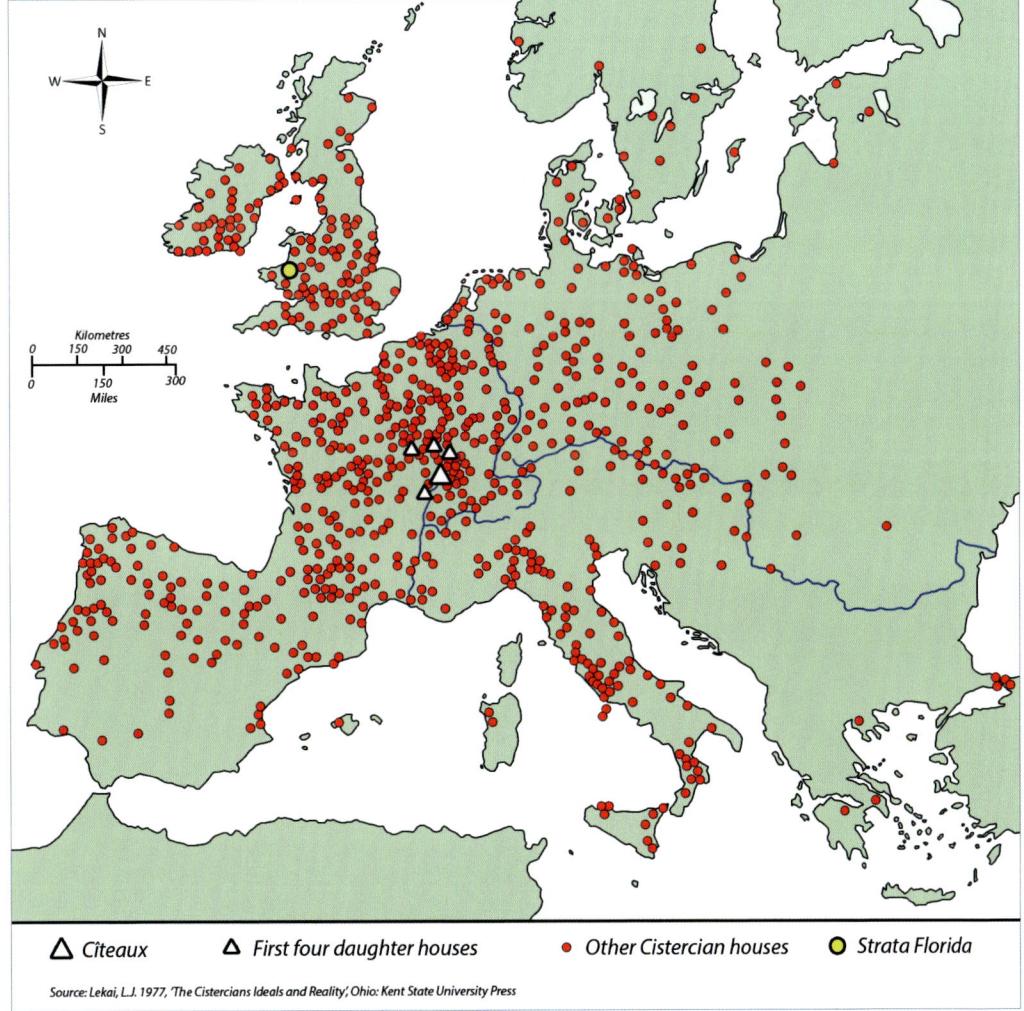

△ Cîteaux   △ First four daughter houses   • Other Cistercian houses   ◯ Strata Florida

Source: Lekai, L.J. 1977, 'The Cistercians Ideals and Reality', Ohio: Kent State University Press

The movement spread from its epicentre in Burgundy to other areas of France, to Italy and the Holy Roman Empire, the newly Christianized lands east of the Elbe, Christian Spain, eastwards to Cyprus and the Holy Land, north to Scandinavia, and, from the end of the 1120s, to England, Wales, Scotland, and Ireland. In the words of a monk of Heisterbach (Germany) the Order was 'transplanted across many seas'. Strata Florida was part of this great story. The nearby women's house at Llanllŷr, with which Strata Florida enjoyed some kind of association, was part of the female narrative. There was, in Wales, a second Cistercian house for women. This was Llanllugan near Montgomery, where a fifteenth-century image of an abbess or nun survives in a restored window.

Fig. 8:
Window in St Mary's church at Llanllugan, Powys, set in the east end wall of the chancel of the former abbey church, now the parish church. This depiction of a nun or abbess dates to the mid fifteenth century.

But we now need to ask: what did Cistercians of this great congregation actually do? Because the normative texts were drawn up for Cistercian houses for men, the following discussion relates to the life of all those who formed their communities: the monks, the monk-officials, and the *conversi* (lay brothers), all of whom are discussed below. Let us look first at how the daily life of the monks was organized.

Fig. 9:
A famous visual expression of the centrality of manual labour for the Cistercian way of life (centre) (Cambridge University Library, MS Mm.5.31, f. 113r).

'Seven Times a Day Have I Given Praise to You … At Midnight I Rose to Give Praise to You'

The Rule of St Benedict laid down a careful structure for the daily life of a monastic community. At its core was the performance of liturgy (church services), which Benedict called *Opus Dei* ('the Work of God)'. Based on Psalm 119 (from which the above quotations from the Rule are drawn) there were seven occasions (or canonical hours) during the day and one during the night, on which the monks gathered in the church for communal worship.

The Canonical Hours

The precise time at which these offices, or services, took place varied with the season of the year, but the day started early, with the night office (Nocturns, also known as Vigils and later as Matins), which began anywhere between 1.30 and 2.30 am. It was important that all the monks should be roused from sleep at the correct time, and the sacrist (the monk who was responsible for the church services) was usually the one charged with this task. The sacrist would have sounded a bell or struck a *tabula* (wooden board) to wake the monks. The monks took the shortest route from their dormitory into the church down the stairs known appropriately as the 'night stairs'. These were generally located in the south transept and an example can be seen, with its handrail, at Neath Abbey in south Wales.

Fig. 10: The night stairs in the ruins of the south transept at Neath Abbey.

The monks were told to encourage each other to move in a seemly fashion, not to hurry, and to be aware of the excuses that sleepyheads might make to try to stay in bed. It could be difficult to keep awake during the night office, and Cistercian cautionary tales related how monks who drifted into sleep were rudely awoken. One monk found himself seized by his cowl (the long-sleeved tunic worn by a monk), hauled to his feet, and warned by the Lord himself to mend his ways. Another less worthy brother, when reprimanded by the precentor for dozing, stormed back to the dormitory in a sulk, and found a troop of screaming demons waiting for him by the latrines. He fainted, was carried to the infirmary – and learned his lesson.

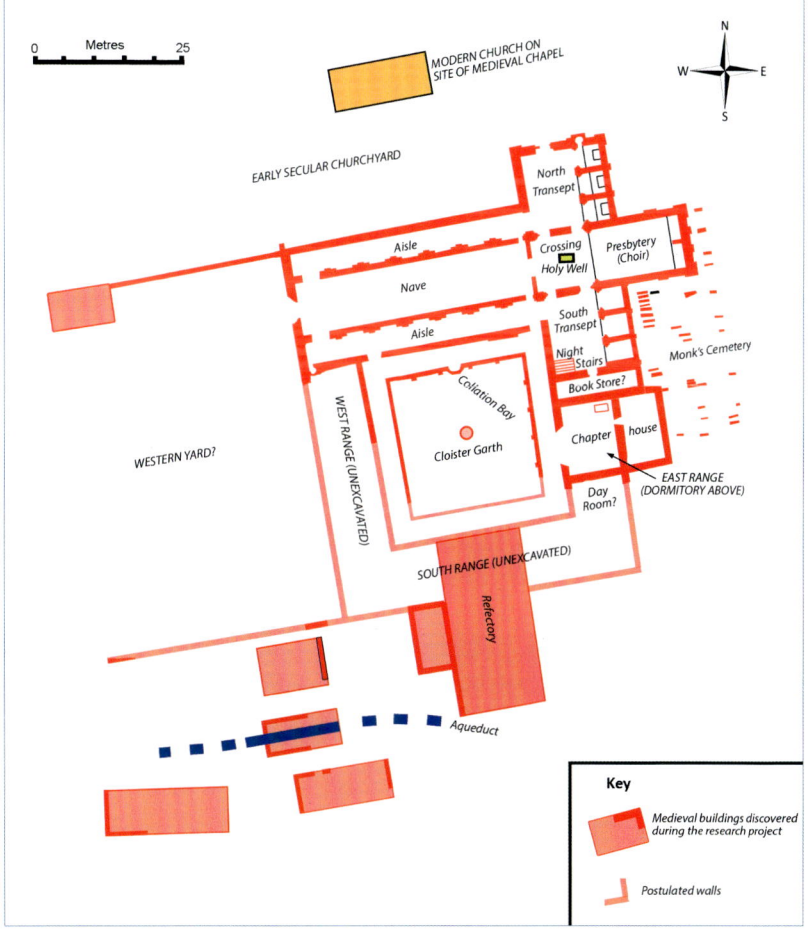

Fig. 11: The architectural framework of monastic religious observance at Strata Florida. This is based on the results of current research, including an attempt to speculate what the complete claustral complex would have looked like in plan. There are still significant unknowns most particularly the southern extent of the east and west ranges.

Nocturns usually lasted about an hour, and there was a short break before the next office of Lauds, which was celebrated as the first light of day appeared in the sky – anywhere between 3.00 am in summer and 7.30 am in winter. During this break, the monks could attend to the 'necessities of nature', or, during the longer interval in winter, could read. Unlike the Benedictines, the Cistercians did not go back to bed between the two offices but remained in church or sat in the cloister reading and meditating. The further offices of Prime (the first hour, sunrise, 4.00 am in summer and 8.00 am in winter), Terce (the third hour), Sext (the sixth hour), None (the ninth hour), and Vespers (the evening office), followed at regular intervals. Each office followed a similar format, beginning with the Lord's Prayer and continuing with hymns, psalms, and chants, all performed under the watchful eyes of the monastic officials known as the cantor (precentor) and subcantor (succentor).

After Vespers the monks gathered in the refectory for a drink before going into church for the final office, Compline, which would have taken place around 8.00 pm in summer and 4.00 pm in winter. This was preceded by a reading, or 'collation'. Benedict recommended that early monument of monastic literature, the *Conferences* of John Cassian (accounts of his visits to the hermit monks of Egypt) or the lives of the Fathers, but warned against parts of the Old Testament because it was not appropriate for 'weak minds' to hear such things at that time of day. The collation allowed monks engaged on special duties to catch up with their fellows before the beginning of Compline. It generally took place in the north range of the cloister where, at Strata Florida, the remains of the collation desk may be seen. After the end of Compline, the abbot sprinkled the brothers with holy water, they put up their hoods and proceeded in silence to the dormitory.

The repeated programme of the offices reminded the monks that this was their primary purpose: everything else in their lives revolved around prayer and worship.

Fig. 12:
Reconstruction painting by Terry Ball of the presbytery or choir at the east end of the Cistercian church at Rievaulx, Yorkshire (copyright: English Heritage).

Masses

Masses, which culminated in the celebration of the Eucharist or Holy Communion, also formed an important part of worship. The Eucharist was – and remains – important for Christians as the celebration that Christ himself instituted at the Last Supper in memory of his own death on the Cross. The Eucharist re-enacted the sharing of bread and wine that Christ gave to his disciples, and the Catholic doctrine of transubstantiation holds that at the moment of consecration these become the body and blood of Christ. Mass was (and is) celebrated by a priest. Cistercian monks took communion every Sunday and on feast days. The mass was celebrated by one of the monks who was ordained to the priesthood. Unlike the Benedictines, the Cistercians discouraged individual monks from seeking ordination, and it is likely that mass was celebrated by the abbot. From the thirteenth century, however, the number of monk priests grew, and those who did not proceed to ordination might be known as lay monks. A conventual high mass was celebrated once a day (after Terce). A second (low) mass was added on Sundays and feast days and included a mass for the dead.

Mass was celebrated at the high altar in the east end of the church. Officials such as the porter might be excused attendance but for others there was no dispensation except for those sick and elderly monks in the infirmary who were not strong enough to sustain its demands. It became customary for monks who were also priests to say a private mass daily, and such masses were requested or expected by founders and benefactors of an abbey for the salvation of their souls. Commemorative prayer was especially valued (that is, prayers on the anniversary of a person's death) and it was for this reason that benefactors were so generous to the Cistercians. Additional altars for these private masses were located in the south and north transepts, and when the number of lay brothers declined parts of the nave might be repurposed to accommodate more altars.

Fig. 13: (left) Central of three chapels on the east side of the south transept at Strata Florida: (right) The bases of two additional altars at the east end of the church behind the high altar.

Performance

The offices were performed in the area of the church known as the monks' choir, which was located in the crossing (where the two arms of the cross-shape of the church intersected) and often, as at Strata Florida, extended into the eastern bays of the nave (the long arm of the cross). At Strata Florida this meant that as the monks chanted the offices, they would have stood around the holy well on two or three sides. In choir the monks positioned themselves according to their seniority within the community, that is, by their date of profession rather than their age. The abbot occupied the first stall on the right-hand (south) side of the choir (nearest the west) and the prior opposite him in the first stall on the left-hand (north) side.

The Cistercians deliberately pared back the elaborate liturgy that had grown up around the canonical hours since Benedict's day and went back to the timetable that he set out. The basis of the offices was the book of Psalms, which formed part of the Old Testament of the Bible, and the entire Psalter (150 Psalms) was recited over the course of a week. They were chanted antiphonally, that is, with each side of the choir taking alternate verses. The Cistercians sought the most authentic form of plainsong (chant) for the offices in order to restore what they saw as primitive rigour. More than one Cistercian writer reminded his fellow monks that they were to avoid musical embellishments, the 'swelling and swooping' of voices, and 'ornaments and trills' on the melody. There was to be no room for showing off musical talents.

The Blessed Virgin Mary in Cistercian Liturgy

The Cistercian Order was noted for its devotion to the Blessed Virgin Mary, the mother of Christ. A Cistercian liturgical innovation was the inclusion of the hymn *Salve regina* which, from the thirteenth century, brought the service of Compline to a close. This was a hymn in praise of the Blessed Virgin Mary. It was to her as 'Queen of Heaven and Earth' that all Cistercian monasteries were dedicated.

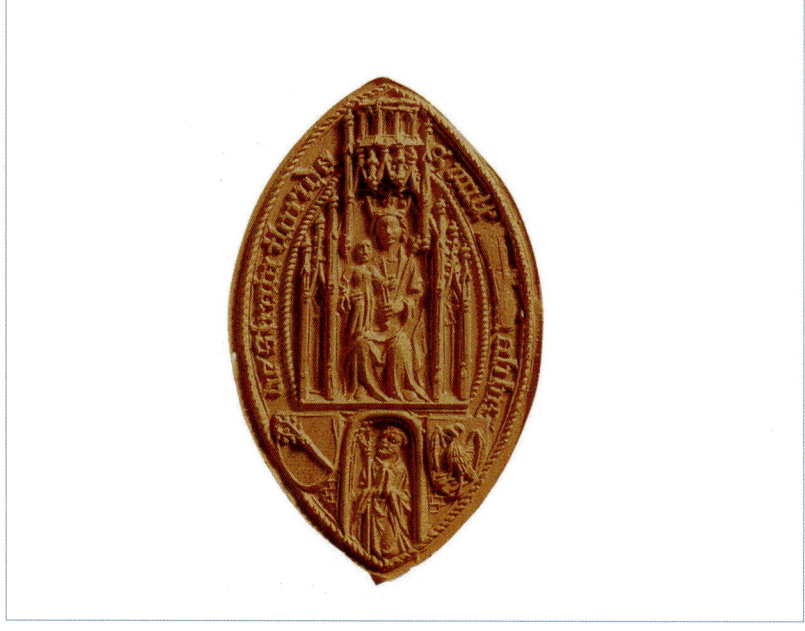

Fig. 14: Seal of Strata Florida, depicting St Mary, the Mother of God, as Queen of Heaven.

> Hail, holy Queen, Mother of Mercy,
> Hail our life, our sweetness and our hope.
> To thee do we cry,
> Poor banished children of Eve;
> To thee do we send up our sighs,
> Mourning and weeping in this valley of tears.
> Turn then, most gracious advocate,
> Thine eyes of mercy toward us;
> And after this our exile,
> Show unto us the blessed fruit of thy womb, Jesus.
> O clement, O loving,
> O sweet Virgin Mary.

Mary was regarded as the special protector of Cistercian monks and nuns, and as such in the late Middle Ages often appears on Cistercian seals and in paintings, sheltering monks and nuns of the order under her cloak.

The Monk of Strata Florida and a Vision in Choir
Cistercian chroniclers of the late twelfth and early thirteenth century tell a story of how one year, on the eve of the feast of Pentecost (Whitsuntide), a monk of Strata Florida rose at the sound of the bell for the night office, and – as required – proceeded into the church. As he chanted, he was filled with new and increased devotion. When the monks began the canticle (song) 'O all ye works of the Lord, bless ye the Lord' he saw a vision of an angel who held a censer (a container for incense) coming in through a window. The angel took the censer to the high altar and censed it, that is, wafted incense over it, and returned to the choir, passing down both sides and censing the monks. When the angel came near, the devout monk opened his mouth, and the angel took a glowing coal from the censer and placed it in the monk's mouth. He then experienced both ecstasy and pain and was taken to the infirmary where he remained as one dead for three days. In one version of the story, the monk was given the ability to see the demons who tempted his fellows – and likely made himself unpopular by revealing those of his brothers who were tempted. In another, the monk was whisked out of the church and carried eastwards in spirit where for a day and a night he experienced visions. His body, meanwhile, was taken to the infirmary by his brothers.

Stories such as these, which circulated widely in the Cistercian world, were intended to teach and instruct: monks learned from them to avoid the snares of temptation and that to be a devout Cistercian brought its spiritual rewards.

The Material Setting of Worship

The physical locus for monastic worship was the church and the cloister that adjoined it. However, before we discuss these, we should note their broader surroundings of both the inner court of the precinct and an outer area comprising enclosures, gardens, orchards, and buildings focused on production of various kinds.

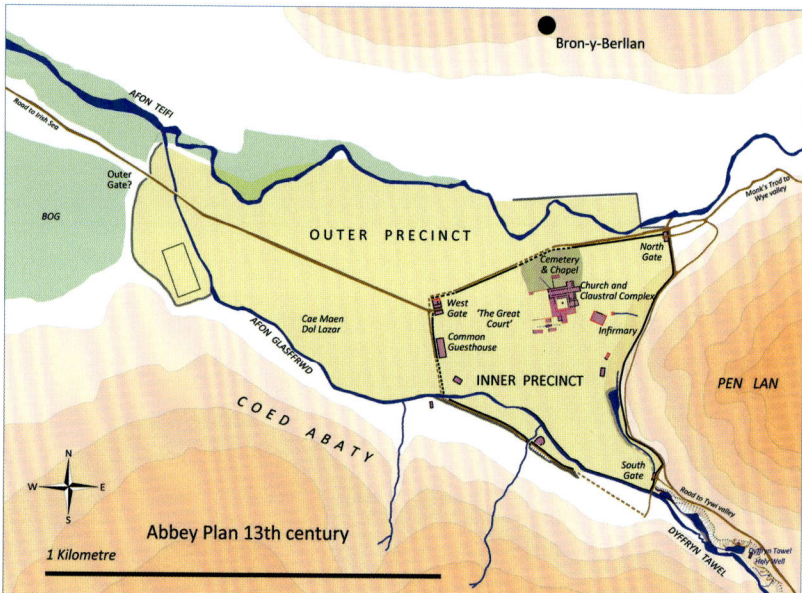

Fig. 15: A reconstruction plan of the layout of Strata Florida's precinct in its early years, although we now know that it retreated from this large extent about a hundred years after the foundation.

Within the church, the Cistercians turned their backs on the ornate, indeed often lavish, material settings of Benedictine liturgy. William of Malmesbury, an English Benedictine monk writing in the 1120s, captured a sense of how Cistercian monasteries were devoid of glittering gold, silver, and gems. This echoed Cistercian regulations which ordered that everything used in the church was to be simple. Like the linen that covered the altar, vestments were not to be of silk. Ornaments, vessels, and utensils for the altar were to be without gold, silver, and jewels. The Cistercians were allowed to have only one chalice and one *fistula* (communion tube) of gold or silver plate. This was a particularly significant object since it was through the fistula that the priest celebrating mass took the precious blood of Christ.

Sculptures and paintings were forbidden because they were thought to distract the monks. One exception was that painted wooden crosses were allowed. St Bernard of Clairvaux in his tract known as the *Apologia*, railed against the excessive size and superfluous decoration of non-Cistercian monastic churches, and the early generations of Cistercian churches were modest in size. Bernard thought that 'soaring heights' and 'unnecessary widths' were a distraction for monks during the offices. To him, they were showy and designed to entice visitors to make financial offerings. Moreover, he argued, while images might be useful in churches used by the laity in order to explain the church's teachings, they were not needed in a Cistercian context in which lay visitors were discouraged.

Fig. 16:
Despite St Bernard's expressed resistance to figurative and decorative sculpture in Cistercian monasteries, this thirteenth-century head, carved in Painswick limestone, was found in the heart of the church at Strata Florida during the nineteenth-century excavations. It appears to be part of a half-sized but full-length portrayal of a tonsured monk. Some have interpreted this as being St Bernard himself.

As a final flourish, Bernard could not justify the expense: churches should not shine with gold when the poor went hungry. In similar vein, Aelred of Rievaulx urged monks to emulate the poverty of Christ and to avoid the sin of curiosity, stimulated by images. which leads to desire and greed.

Bernard's and Aelred's opinions chimed with early Cistercian legislation, but it is important to remember that in such a large monastic order there was variation in practice from an early date. Moreover, it would be a mistake to think that the material setting of monastic churches did not change with changing times and fashions. Although some (usually smaller and poorer houses) show little evidence of rebuilding apart from necessary repair and perhaps contraction of the original plans, at others both churches and claustral buildings might be reconstructed on a larger scale and more ambitious design. A good example is Tintern, where Abbot John decided, in 1269, to rebuild the abbey church.

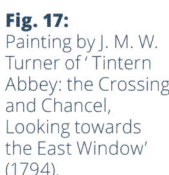

Fig. 17: Painting by J. M. W. Turner of 'Tintern Abbey: the Crossing and Chancel, Looking towards the East Window' (1794).

By 1288 the work had progressed far enough for the monks to occupy the new choir, and by 1301 – with the financial aid of Tintern's patron, Roger Bigod – the new church was dedicated. In design it would have been very different from its predecessor, and embellishments continued to be made for another half century. For several decades the Tintern monks would have carried on their daily routine in what might have resembled a building site. Their experience would not have been uncommon. The late fourteenth-century chronicle of Meaux Abbey in Yorkshire makes it clear that there would not have been a time in the abbey's history to the date of writing when some building activity was not taking place.

Moving around the Church and Cloisters: Rituals and Processions

Not all the liturgy was static, and rituals and processions were an important part of monastic life. Liturgical activities such as these were performed throughout the Cistercian world, and both enhanced worship and reinforced a sense of Cistercian community across Christendom. In tune with the general Cistercian trend to curtail the blossoming of the liturgy that had occurred during the tenth and eleventh centuries, the number of processions was reduced in early Cistercian worship, but then multiplied in the course of the thirteenth century.

Annual Processions

The earliest Processions (recorded by the middle of the twelfth century) were those that commemorated some of the key festivals of the Church's year: Palm Sunday, the Sunday before Easter, which marked the beginning of Holy Week, was, like Easter a moveable feast; Candlemas, also known as the Purification of the Blessed Virgin Mary (2 February) was an important feast in the developing devotion to Mary; Ascension, the occasion on which Christ rose into heaven was, again, a moveable feast. In 1223 a fourth joined these three: the Assumption of the Blessed Virgin Mary (15 August) which celebrated Mary's reception and coronation in heaven, was another manifestation of devotion to the Mother of God. On these occasions guests and lay people were allowed into the church.

Fig. 18: Reconstruction painting of the monks in procession on Palm Sunday, just about to enter the west door of Strata Florida Abbey (Terry Ball) from the Cadw guide book.

Much of what we know of these rituals derives from the Cistercian customary called the *Ecclesiastica officia* – a customary was a directory of usages relating to the liturgical arrangements, daily life, and administration of a monastery or order. *Ecclesiatica officia* laid down in some detail what was to happen during these ceremonies, and when, and where. On Palm Sunday before the office of Terce, the sacristan placed palm branches on a small table which was set on the presbytery step, that is, to the east of the monks' choir leading up to the high altar. At Strata Florida this would have been to the east of the holy well. The branches were in commemoration of the palms laid down by the people of Jerusalem before Christ as he rode into the city on a donkey at the beginning of the week that culminated in his death (Mark 11:1–11). After the office had ended, the abbot took up the crozier (his staff), blessed the palms, and sprinkled them with holy water. The cantor (the monk in charge of the performance of the offices) then offered one branch to the abbot and began the antiphon, during which the sacrist distributed branches to the monks and novices. If there were any left over, they were given to the lay brothers (**conversi**) and *familia* (household, hired labour), and any guests.

The procession then began. A subdeacon that is, a monk in holy orders, below the rank of deacon) carried the holy water, followed by a deacon (a monk in holy orders, below the rank of priest) bearing an unveiled cross, and by the monks in the same sequence as they stood in choir. Various antiphons were sung and stops made at specified points. The first station, or stopping point, was on the stretch of the cloister walk by the monks' dormitory (located in the east range); the second was by the refectory (in the south range); and the final one was by the church (the north cloister walk). While various rituals were performed there, the sacrist went to the chapter house and fetched the Gospel text, bringing it to the entrance into the church.

Fig. 19:
The remains of the north cloister walk at Strata Florida, looking east. To the left is the south aisle of the church and ahead is the south transept with (under modern canopies) small chapels. To the right (south) of this is a narrow room, likely to be a vestry and/or a bookstore, and further south still, the ruins of the chapter house. The ruins of the collation bay (discussed above) can be seen about halfway along the cloister wall to the south (right).

The gospel was read by the deacon who faced east, with his back to the monks. To the singing of further antiphons, the monks re-entered the church through the west door and, on reaching the choir, laid their branches on the steps of the presbytery (east end). If there were any lay people present, they did not take part in the procession in the cloister or enter the chapter house – though exceptions could be made for persons 'of venerable standing'.

Candlemas was another important feast in the veneration of the Blessed Virgin Mary. It fell forty days after Christmas and commemorated the presentation by Mary of Christ in the Temple (Luke 2:22–38). The Cistercian liturgy required that candles be brought in advance to the presbytery so that the abbot could bless them with holy water. Candles were then distributed in much the same way as palm branches. The procession also followed the same pattern – as indeed it did for the Ascension celebration, which was forty days after Easter (Acts 1:9).

The Weekly Ritual: the Blessing of the Water

The 'Blessing of Holy Water' (*benedictio aque*) was the important Sunday ritual that preceded high (conventual) Mass and was attended by the whole community. It was intended as a celebration of the internal landscape of the cloister. In preparation, a small table was placed on the presbytery step, with salt, water, and a sprinkler. The priest approached the presbytery step holding the appropriate liturgical book and blessed the salt and the water. He then walked all the way around the high altar and shook water droplets on it; he then did the same in the presbytery. A senior office-holding monk took some of the water and processed around the cloister, in turn sprinkling the cloister and the rooms off it in specified order: chapter house, parlour, dormitory, with attached latrine, warming room, refectory, kitchen, cellarer's storeroom (usually on the ground floor of the west range, below the dormitory of the *conversi*). If there was any water left, he poured it into the holy water receptacle at the west entrance to the church.

Meanwhile, the priest stood on the presbytery step and sprinkled each member of the community, in this order: the abbot, the priest himself, the ministers, the choir monks (in the order they stood in choir, which reflected seniority), the novices, and the *conversi* or lay brothers (on whom see below). Then the sacristan picked up the basin of holy water and took it to the part of the church reserved for the guests and *familia*. He did not sprinkle them but offered the vessel into which they dipped their fingers to bless themselves.

Fig. 20:
An unusual feature of the liturgical layout at Strata Florida is this stone-lined cistern set into the floor of the crossing, just in front of the presbytery step (marked by a low bank) with the high altar beyond (to the right). It is plumbed into the abbey's main water supply which originates at an elaborate holy well up-stream. The water flowed into and out of a small, square, stone-lined basin with steps leading down to it from the east and the west. The upper edge of the feature has a recess which looks to have housed a trapdoor or other covering. This has been interpreted as a holy well and may be related to the *benedictio aque* described above. Such a feature is not known at any other Cistercian monastery, although there is a direct parallel in the same position at a Benedictine abbey at Landevennec in Brittany.

As noted above, that part of this ritual involved one of the monks leaving the church and scattering the cloister and its rooms (in a specific order) with salt and water. This may have a bearing on the spatial organization of the claustral buildings, in particular the arrangement of the refectory. The evidence is that in early Cistercian monasteries the refectory was laid out on an east/west axis (that is, parallel to the church), which is likely to have meant that the kitchen lay outside the cloister. In houses, such as Strata Florida, however, which were founded or constructed from about the middle of the twelfth century onwards, refectories seem to have been designed from the beginning to run on a north/south axis. At sites such as Fountains and Rievaulx, the older refectories were replaced so that they would conform to this newer layout. This may simply reflect a growth in numbers: if a community built east-west there was no real way to expand if a larger refectory was needed, whereas building north/south meant expansion to the south was much more feasible. However, that does not explain why even modest houses built to conform to this new plan. It has been argued that the reason behind the rethink was to bring the kitchen firmly into the cloister, so that it became part of the landscape blessed with holy water in this weekly ritual.

The Maundy (*mandatum*)

The *mandatum* or maundy recalled the episode recorded in the gospel when at the Last Supper Christ washed the feet of his apostles (John 13: 4–12). Within the Christian tradition the Last Supper was a highly charged and significant event. It was the final time that Christ and his disciples were together, when Christ foretold that he would be betrayed by one of them, and when he instituted the Eucharist (Communion) with the breaking of bread and blessing of wine which were his body and blood (Matthew 26:17–30; Mark 14:12–26; Luke 22: 14–23; John 13: 1–20). After the supper and washing of the feet of the disciples, Christ was betrayed by Judas Iscariot, tried, and crucified the following day (Good Friday). The monastic *mandatum* commemorated and recalled these events and in particular Christ's command to his followers that they should love one another.

There were two monastic ceremonies with similar names: the *mandatum fratrum*, the maundy of the brothers, and the *mandatum hospitum*, the maundy of the guests. These are mentioned respectively in chapters 35 and 53 of the Rule of St Benedict. The *mandatum hospitum* relates to the washing of the feet of guests, and precise details are laid down in the Cistercian *Ecclesiastica officia*. Each Saturday during the daily chapter two monks were delegated for the following week to perform the *mandatum* for such guests as would arrive during that period. When summoned to greet the guest(s) they went in procession to the guest house. Part of their welcome was to wash the feet of their visitors there.

The *mandatum fratrum* took place weekly, on a Saturday, and the rite was performed by the outgoing and incoming monk servers of meals for the week. The Rule of St Benedict is quite brief on the maundy of the brothers and does not specify a location where it was to take place. In Benedictine houses such as Farfa (Italy) the location was the chapter house, but the Cistercians moved it to the entrance to the refectory. The *Ecclesiastica officia* gives full details of the rituals. There were a number of reasons why this location was particularly appropriate. Water was readily available there. The *lavatorium* or laver (troughs), placed on the outer wall of the refectory within the south cloister walk and usually supplied by pipes, provided water for the monks to wash their hands before meals. The *lavatorium* was also the locus of the weekly maundy. In places such as Fountains Abbey and Rievaulx Abbey traces have been detected of a bench positioned above or behind the troughs on which the monks might sit and dangle their feet (though making sure that for decency's sake their feet remained covered by their habit). The importance of the location explains the architectural splendour that we find, for instance, at Tintern, Hailes (Gloucestershire) and Cleeve (Somerset). On the continent the *lavatorium* might be a free-standing structure off the south cloister walk opposite the refectory, and really spectacular examples can be seen at Cistercian Mellifont (Ireland) and the Cluniac priory of Much Wenlock (Shropshire).

Fig. 21: Elaborate *lavatoria* at (above) Poblet (Catalunya) and (below) Mellifont (Ireland).

The architectural setting and location for the *mandatum* had a symbolic value. By the twelfth century it was held that Christ washed the feet of the apostles in a room below the upper chamber in which the Last Supper took place. Thus, in some Cistercian monasteries such as Byland and Rievaulx the refectory was on an upper floor and symbolized the upper room of the Last Supper. Below was an undercroft at the entrance to which the *mandatum* took place. Even without this more elaborate setting, the *mandatum* was above all else a re-enactment of the Last Supper and an example of charity and humility.

The *mandatum fratrum* was expanded on Maundy Thursday when it was performed by the abbot and monks and became the central liturgical act of the day. At the hour of Sext, the gatekeeper chose poor men, the same number as there were monks in the monastery at that time. These poor men waited in a designated place until summoned. During the chanting of None they were escorted into the cloister by *conversi*. They took off their shoes and sat in line in the north cloister alley (next to the church), beginning from the door by which the monks normally entered the cloister (this was in the corner of the cloister and the south transept).

The *conversi* then fetched basins and towels. When None had finished the monks came into the cloister, led by the abbot. When the abbot reached the last of the poor men (the one furthest away from the door into the church) he and the monks performed the *mandatum* – hence the need to match the numbers of poor men to monks, so that each monk could minister to one man. Each monk washed the feet of a poor man and also gave him money. At the end of the ceremony the poor men were led out of the cloister to the guest house where they were fed.

There was yet another part to the Maundy Thursday commemorations. Before the meal certain monks were designated to heat and bring water to the cloister. After a short interval following the meal, the monks returned to the refectory, each to his own seat, and were joined by the *conversi*. The abbot, wearing a linen apron, washed the feet of four monks, four novices, and four lay brothers (if there were not enough novices, then the deficit was made up by *conversi*). The remainder was attended to by the abbot's helpers, while they themselves were washed by the abbot. The abbot was the last to receive this service. While stressing the virtues of charity and humility, the maundy ritual cemented the bonds of community and of love (*caritas*) which was a keystone of Cistercian monasticism.

The Dedication Ceremonies
It is notable that many Cistercian churches have finely decorated west ends, which might be enhanced by a porch or narthex, known as a galilee. Galilee was the biblical land of Jesus's life, teaching, and miracles, and the place where he met his disciples after his resurrection. The term 'galilee' suggests that passing through the Cistercian church enacted Christ's ministry. The galilee was also sometimes known as the Paradise porch; as we shall see, the Cistercian monastery and in particular the cloister were associated with paradise.

The galilee was a popular place of burial for benefactors and special friends of a monastery, particularly in the early decades when burial within the church was discouraged. A fine example of a galilee can be seen at Fountains Abbey, and at Rievaulx eight burials have survived in the porch. The most likely explanation for the architectural elaboration of the west door is that it played a part in processions – witness the fine examples from Strata Florida and Valle Crucis.

Fig. 22:
The west portal of Strata Florida church expressed in a Transitional style of architecture, but adorned, around its edges, with motifs drawn from regional, pre-Cistercian (so-called 'Celtic') artforms.

At Byland the great circular opening above the west door once contained a large rose window, roses being symbolic of the Virgin Mary. The west end is not mentioned much in written sources, but it would have been a primary station in guest processions: a visiting abbot or bishop, for instance, would have been greeted by the whole community at the gate and then conducted through the main (west) door of the church, up the nave (the choir of the *conversi*) and the monks' choir to the high altar. The west end also had an important function in dedication ceremonies.

Fig. 23:
This piece of Dundry (Jurassic) limestone once formed part of the main portal arch rubble of the Strata Florida western gatehouse. Found during excavations in 2010, it has been eroded by its time in the very acidic soils of Strata Florida, but a cross can be clearly seen incised into the surface in such a position that it was visible at eye level to visitors and monks alike, perhaps during the annual dedication ceremony, although it was found at a considerable distance from the church.

The annual dedication ceremony, marking the anniversary of the dedication of a Cistercian church, was one of the few processions that involved monks leaving the inner cloister. It involved a threefold circumambulation of, or walk around, the church and a triumphal entry through the west door. Traces of the ceremony can – if we are lucky – be found in the 'twelve crosses painted or carved on the interior walls around the periphery of the church' (eleven survive from the French monastery of Sénanque). During the ceremony a candle would be attached to each cross and it would be sprinkled with holy oil. The crosses seem to have been placed as follows: two on the west wall of the nave, facing pairs along the nave walls and transept ends, and the others around the east end.

Let us now revisit the cloister and think about what monks did there when they were not in church.

The Cloister: the Heart of the Community

The cloister was an open space surrounded by a walkway on all four sides; it lay physically and symbolically at the heart of the monastery. It was usually (though not always) placed to the south of the church to take advantage of the natural light. In Wales, an important exception can be seen at Tintern, where the cloister and related buildings lay to the north of the church, an arrangement dictated by the location of the river Wye in relation to the land granted by Walter fitz Richard de Clare for the establishment of the monastery.

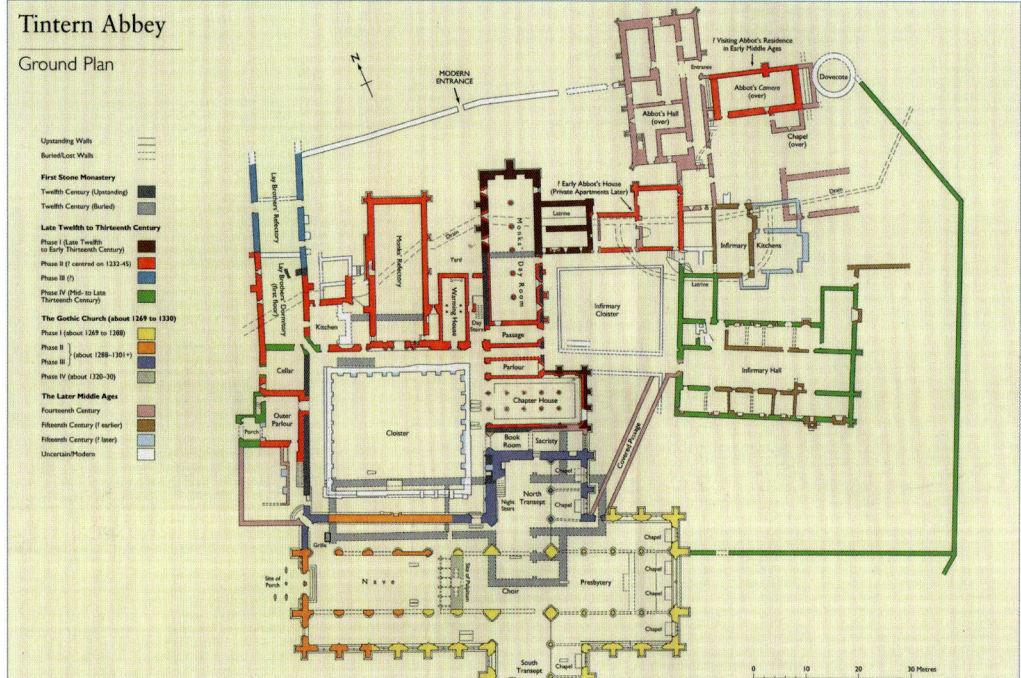

Fig. 24: Plan of Tintern Abbey in Monmouthshire.

For Cistercian monks the cloister had a symbolic as well as a practical importance: it was a place of quiet contemplation and reflection and was seen as a foretaste of Paradise. In his life of Aelred, abbot of Cistercian Rievaulx (1147–67), Walter Daniel likened the entire monastery to Paradise, speaking of the hills and trees encircling the abbey like a crown as providing the monks with 'a second paradise of wooded delight'. In his treatise entitled *Spiritual Friendship* Aelred himself described walking around the cloister of his abbey. The brothers, he said, were sitting around forming 'a most loving crown'; in the middle were trees containing fruit, leaves, and flowers, 'the delights of paradise'. A story of the foundation of Jervaulx Abbey, daughter house of Byland (both also in Yorkshire) told how the abbot who was about to leave Byland to establish a daughter house at Jervaulx had a vision in which a fair woman held a beautiful boy by his hand as he plucked a branch from a small tree in the centre of the cloister. Later, when the abbot and his monks were lost in a dense wood, the woman and child – the Blessed Virgin Mary and Christ – appeared to them and the child, holding the same branch, guided them to safety and their new home. The natural beauty of the trees, flowers, and fruit may have recalled the Garden of Eden before the Fall of humankind.

Fig. 25:
The 'Paradise' of Strata Florida, looking eastwards. In the foreground is the precinct of the abbey, the inner gatehouse of which can be seen under excavation. At the centre are the buildings of Mynachlog Fawr and the Cadw monument of church and cloisters. To the right are the Abbey Wood and the valley of the Afon Glasffrwd. Behind and to the east of Mynachlog Fawr is the hill of Pen-lan where there are extensive earthworks of agricultural use. Beyond that, in the distance, are the Cambrian Mountains.

Off the east, south, and west walkways of the cloister lay all the rooms that were necessary for the daily life of the monks.

The Daily Chapter: the Greatest and the Least

When the office of Prime was over, the monks left church by the door at the south-east angle of the cloister and entered the chapter house for the daily meeting under the presidency of the abbot. Here they sat on benches set against the walls while the abbot took his place at the lectern (reading desk). Proceedings began with a reading of a chapter of the Rule of St Benedict (hence the name of the room). The daily chapter was the forum for the confession of faults and the imposition of penance, as well as commemoration of deceased brothers and benefactors. It was also where the monks discussed any business of the community. This might concern the abbot's forthcoming attendance at the General Chapter at Cîteaux, or the visitation of daughter houses; whether new buildings or repairs were needed either at the abbey or on its granges; whether to accept an offer of land from a benefactor; or consideration of requests for confraternity or burial. On major feast days the abbot would preach a sermon during the chapter. Important personages might be received in the chapter house, having first waited in the parlour (a room where talking was allowed), which generally lay to the south of the chapter house, on the ground floor of the east range. Benedict's Rule reminded the abbot that in all these matters he was to remember that, although in terms of precedence he was the greatest of all within his abbey, he was to take the advice of even the least of his monks.

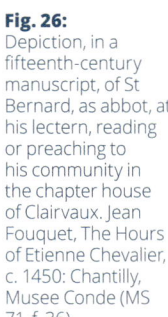

Fig. 26:
Depiction, in a fifteenth-century manuscript, of St Bernard, as abbot, at his lectern, reading or preaching to his community in the chapter house of Clairvaux. Jean Fouquet, The Hours of Etienne Chevalier, c. 1450: Chantilly, Musee Conde (MS 71, f. 36).

Yet it would be a mistake to think of the chapter house simply as a place of routine meetings and business. It was, after the church, the most important building in the complex. It was about community, authority, and corporate memory. It was customary, at least in the twelfth and thirteenth century and in some cases later, for abbots to be buried in the chapter house. In this way, they remained a part of the community, a link with the past, and a reminder to present and future abbots of the weight of their authority and their responsibility for the welfare of their monks. A relatively complete chapter house (though lacking its benches) can be seen at Valle Crucis.

Fig. 27:
Interior of the chapter house at Valle Crucis, near Llangollen, in north Wales.

A Balanced Day: Reading and Work; Sleeping and Eating

We have seen how the recitation of the regular offices of the day formed the most important part of a monk's day. In writing his Rule, however, Benedict was concerned to balance prayer with other activities so that his monks did not become subject to the sin of boredom, or lack of concentration. The Cistercians were keen to return to the strict observance of the Rule, so they made certain that parts of the day were set aside for 'sacred reading' (*lectio divina*) and others for work.

Reading

Though local arrangements might vary, it was often in the cloister walkways, particularly on the north abutting the church, that we would have found the desks or carrels at which monks sat to engage in their daily reading and contemplation. At the beginning of Lent each monk collected a book from the book cupboard which he spent a whole year reading. Here we must understand that 'reading' did not mean a cursory read through a book, but slow, deliberate reading and contemplation on the sacred word. Monks read out loud to concentrate the mind on the content of the book.

It was because monks often sat in the cloister to read that St Bernard, the most influential and vocal of twelfth-century Cistercians, held the firm view that the cloister walks should be devoid of all inappropriate sculpture that might distract the monks, citing 'filthy monkeys and fierce lions, fearful centaurs and striped tigers'. In Aelred's *Mirror of Charity* these became 'cranes and hares, does and stags, magpies and ravens'. Lest they disturb their brothers, monks were to sit one behind the other so that they could not talk or otherwise communicate, and they had their hoods down so that they could not have a quiet snooze. During the long daylight hours of summer, they were allowed to lie on their beds and read – as long as they did not disturb their fellows.

Fig. 28:
The cloister arcade and a Cistercian monk deep in his chosen text. This image is taken from an important book on monasticism by Thomas Merton, *Silence in Heaven*.

In the cloister, too, they might have taken advantage of the natural light to copy manuscripts. A tale from the life of St Godric, a twelfth-century monk of Durham Cathedral Priory who dwelt in its nearby hermitage at Finchale, warns of the perils of leaving work unattended. A monk of Fountains Abbey was busy copying the life of the saint from a manuscript the abbey had borrowed from Durham when, hearing the bell for the office, he hurried into church. On his return he found that it had been raining hard and, coming in through the unglazed windows, the rain had ruined the manuscript. A quick prayer to the saint brought about its restoration.

Work

Work – termed in the Rule *labor manuum* or 'manual labour' – could take various forms, and, as we will see, for some monks, work would have been less manual and more administrative or managerial. Others would have been engaged in a variety of tasks, such as sweeping, cleaning, and chopping wood. A day room generally

Fig. 29:
An altarpiece by Jörg Breu the Elder (1500) at Zwettl Abbey (Lower Austria): a scene from the Life of St Bernard depicting Cistercian monks harvesting.

located in the east cloister walk provided a venue for occupations such as sewing and mending, making candlesticks, and weaving mats, and provided another location where manuscripts could be copied.

There were regular periods of the day set aside for work but on feast days manual labour gave way to an extended liturgy and reading. On the other hand, there were times when work was a priority. As we see in the late twelfth- and early thirteenth-century *Exordium magnum*, compiled by Conrad, a Cistercian monk of Eberbach (Germany) – a book which is part history, part legendary, part miracle collection – in many Cistercian houses at harvest time the monks would be expected to be out in the fields gathering in the crops.

If they were not able to reach the church, they recited the offices as they worked. Conrad included in the *Exordium magnum* tales of how the monks were encouraged in their physical toils by visits from the Blessed Virgin Mary and other saints, who moved among them and even occasionally wiped their brows. Such tales sanctified the act of labour. For the Cistercians the restoration of manual labour to the daily timetable marked a return to the Rule of St Benedict and reversed the process by which, by the tenth and eleventh centuries, it had lost out to an extended liturgy and a prevailing sense that manual work was inappropriate for monks. Moreover, work had both an economic value and a value as a lesson in humility. All monks were equal and had to serve each other like members of a family.

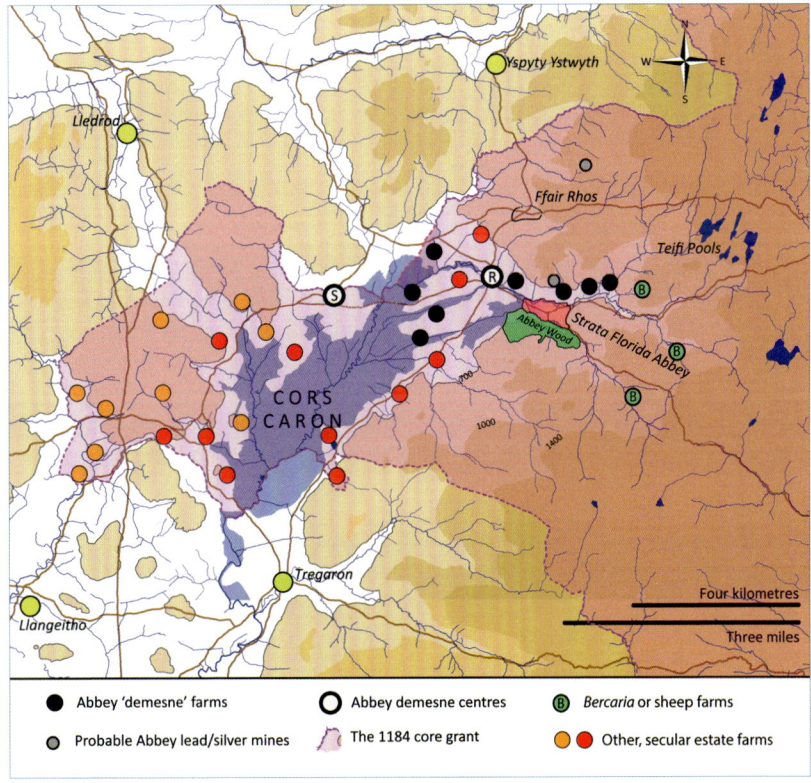

Fig. 30:
The landscape context for the work of the monks at Strata Florida. Here there appears to have been, unlike most other Cistercian abbeys, a 'demesne' or 'mansus' of farms whose place-names still today appear to show that each was a specialised unit focusing on a specific agrarian product. These seem to have been managed from two centres (bond settlements) at Rhydfendigaid (R) and Swyddffynnon (S). Abbey Wood would have been managed by the monks for building and heating materials. Peat for fuel was taken from Cors Caron and elsewhere, and fish and wildfowl from Cors Caron and Teifi Pools. Sheep were farmed from *bercaria* (sheep farms) whose earthworks lie on the mountain edge to the east of the abbey. In the hills around there were also lead mines using new hydraulic engineering introduced by the Cistercians, and also employed for demesne mills.

As the tale from Fountains Abbey demonstrates, for some monks, manual labour would be to write or copy texts. Service books were always required and from time to time these would need to be repaired or replaced. The 'Charter of Love' (*Carta caritatis*), containing administrative arrangements such as the organization of the General Chapter and the annual visitation, stipulated that all Cistercian houses were to use the same liturgical books, such as the missal (mass book), book of collects (prayers), chants for mass, antiphonary (words and music for various psalms and songs), hymnal, and psalter (book of Psalms). When a new monastery was founded, these would be supplied by the mother house – in the case of Strata Florida, from Whitland Abbey – and copied faithfully down the years. It was not just liturgical texts that were copied but works of devotion for the periods of *lectio divina*. The Life of St Godric would have provided suitable material. In addition, Cistercian monasteries would have had the key Cistercian texts: the *Carta caritatis* ('Charter of Love'), the *Ecclesiastica officia* (liturgical requirements and duties of various office holders), and the official histories of the Order that lent a sense of identity to its widely dispersed houses.

At most monasteries at some stage in their history all the original charters (written records of lands and privileges granted to the community) and other legal documents were copied into a volume, known as a cartulary, for easy reference and as a permanent record. At some, however, – including Strata Florida – such a cartulary if it ever existed has not survived the passage of time and might have gone astray when the monastery was suppressed. Within Wales original charters in some numbers survive from Strata Marcella and Margam Abbeys. A monk – or perhaps a team of monks – would be selected to remove charters from the chests and bundles in which they were stored, decide how they were to be arranged within a volume, copy them carefully, and then restore them to the archive.

Cistercian monks – in Wales particularly those of Strata Florida and Valle Crucis – performed an important role in the copying of vernacular Welsh manuscripts, and it is to them that we owe the preservation of much of the corpus of medieval Welsh poetry. Others engaged in original composition or translation, either of chronicles – the *Brut y Tywysogion*, for instance, at Strata Florida and Valle Crucis – or annals (records of yearly events) at Margam in south Wales, or Waverley (Surrey). Some abbots, such as John of York of Fountains (1203–1211), commissioned a history of their own house: John's eye fell on Hugh, a monk of one of his daughter houses, Kirkstall, to undertake the task, possibly because he had already written a history of that abbey.

Fig. 31:
A page from the Hendregadredd manuscript (NLW MS 6680), almost certainly written at Strata Florida in the later thirteenth century by one scribe (known as 'Alpha' by modern scholars). It was later added to and was designed to preserve some of the most important poems in the Welsh language. Folio 79r (image 161) shows the beginning of a poem by Gwynfardd Brycheiniog to St David.

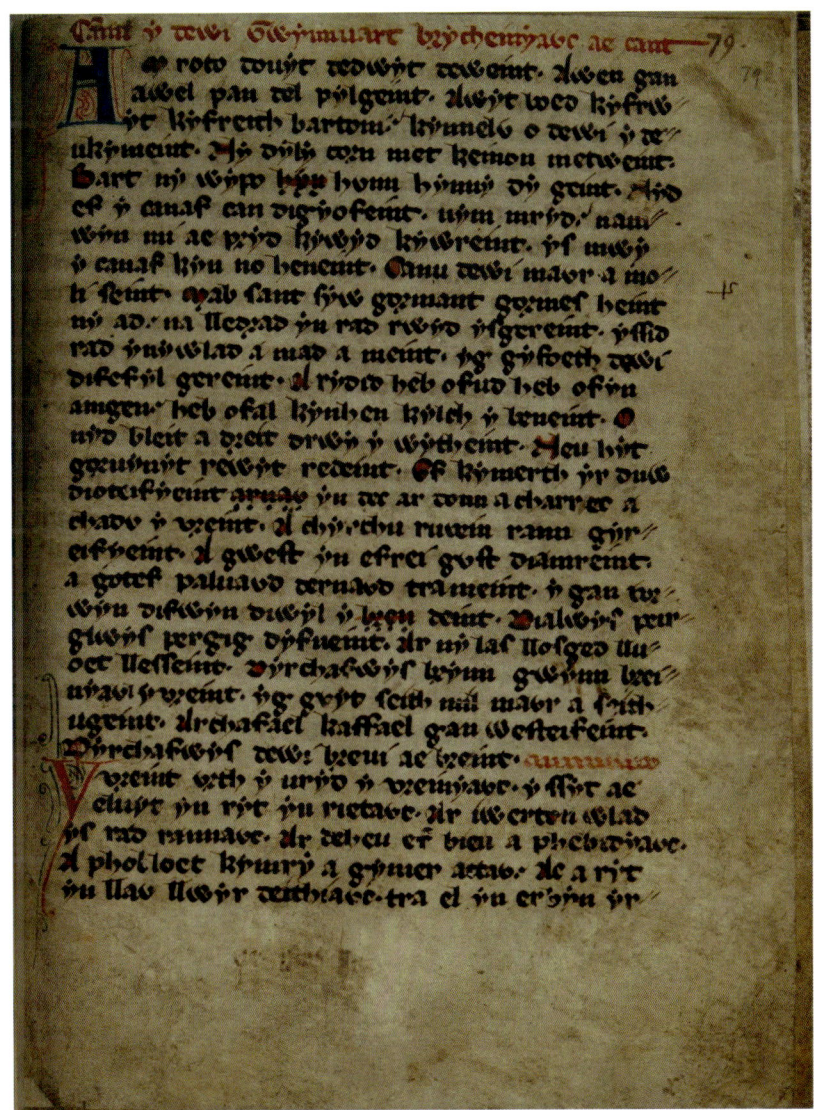

Resting the Body

The monks slept in a common dormitory which, for convenience, was located on the first floor of the east range. There were two entrances or exits. During the daytime the dormitory would have been accessed from a staircase in the east range leading up from the cloister. The monks would have used these stairs if, as the Rule of St Benedict allowed, they wished to have an afternoon nap in summer when the days were longer, or read silently, to avoid disturbing others. At night, however, the monks left the dormitory using the night stairs at the north end which led directly into the church.

Fig. 32: Reconstruction painting of the monks descending the night stairs at Tintern for the office of Nocturns (Terry Ball) from the Cadw guide book.

The monks slept on pallets with their heads against the wall and their feet facing inwards. There was little privacy, although by the later Middle Ages some abbeys had partitioned the dormitory into separate cells, as happened at Cleeve Abbey (Somerset). There was only minimal lighting – one lamp would illuminate the way to the latrines at the south end of the dormitory. The monk whose task it was (on rota) to remain awake would encourage his sleepy brothers to rouse themselves for the night office – and not to fall asleep again. In order to leave his bed quickly a monk slept fully clothed, though having taken the precaution of removing his belt and knife first so that he did not inadvertently roll over and cut himself. This was a mark of Benedict's careful thought and consideration for his monks – a real forerunner of Health and Safety at Work.

There was another reason for remaining clothed. It was important for monks that, should they die during the night, they should be dressed in their habit, ready to meet their maker. To reinforce this point, Caesarius of Heisterbach told a story of a monk of Fossa Nova (Italy) whose brothers had removed his habit to relieve his fever. He died, but almost immediately came back to life to inform the community that he had been turned away from the gates of Paradise because he was not wearing his habit. Once this was restored, he passed away peacefully. In order to demonstrate the maintenance of discipline on the matter of clothing, Caesarius told another tale of a monk who was about to be elected abbot. This was prevented by a vision which warned against the election of a monk who had once slept without his socks.

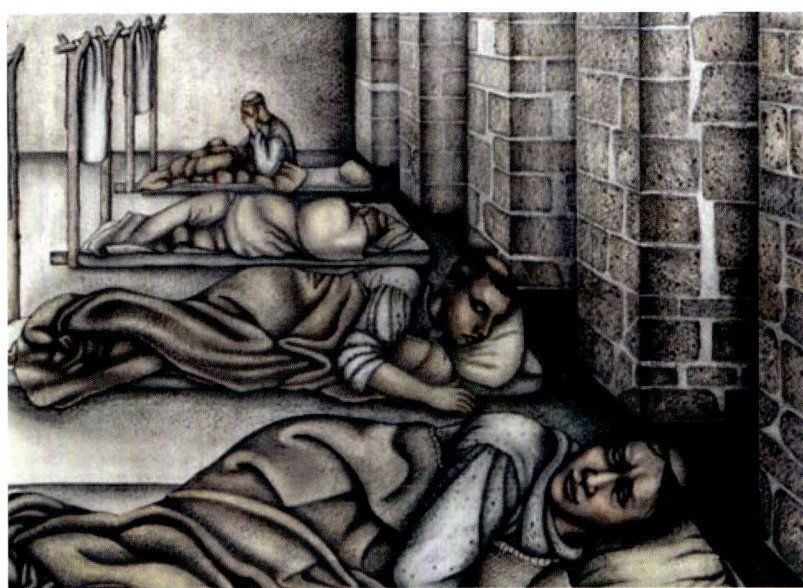

Fig. 33:
Monks sleeping in the dormitory above the east range of the cloisters.

The night could bring terrors and temptation and monks had to remain vigilant, even in sleep, to avoid falling into doubt or sin. One of Bernard's friends, William of St Thierry, advised monks to think of something that would allow them to fall asleep peacefully and remain asleep. That advice must have been easier to read or hear than it was to put into practice, when an unexpected sound from outside, or a nightmare, might keep a monk awake in the hours between Compline and the night office. As a cure for insomnia, Matthew of Rievaulx recommended (silent) recitation of the Athanasian Creed (a statement of Christian belief) seven times, or the seven penitential psalms, which are notable for their expression of sorrow for sins committed. Confession helped, too, as it would have cleared the mind of regret and remorse for offences committed or imagined.

Dangers lay in attempting to communicate with fellow monks, and for this reason the rule of silence was absolute. Both the single light burning and the vigilance of the monks who patrolled the dormitory guarded against improper conduct, but the devil was always at work, and particularly prone to tempt the sleepy or the sleeping. Walter Daniel records how on one occasion the devil visited two monks of Rievaulx during the night. In their terror they bellowed like bulls and awoke the whole convent, which was sufficient to defeat the devil – on this occasion. Monks might be helped to withstand the 'perils and dangers' of the night by visitations from the Blessed Virgin Mary or other saints. At Dunfermline Abbey (Scotland) a monk was saved by St Margaret of Scotland from demons in the form of savage dogs.

Feeding Body and Soul: Food and Drink

Meals were taken in a common refectory, generally located in the south range of the cloister. The Cistercian diet was frugal. A twelfth-century monk of Rievaulx Abbey in Yorkshire wrote of how the Cistercians consumed only what was necessary to maintain the needs of the body: 'a pound of bread, a pint of drink, two dishes of cabbages and beans', though plenty of fresh vegetables were available. The Cistercians consciously returned to the Rule of St Benedict, which specified that only one meal a day should be taken but in summer, in the longer hours of sunlight, a second meal, a light supper, was allowed. At the main meal two dishes (cereal or vegetable based) were served – in case a monk did not like one of them – and extra vegetables and fruit were allowed. Bread was to be coarse (although finer bread was allowed to the sick) and, until restrictions were lifted in the fourteenth century, meat, that is the flesh of four-legged animals, was forbidden.

Fig. 34: The Nanteos Cup. Made of wych-hazel, this is part of a fourteenth-century mazer cup, a vessel which was common on monastic dining tables and in kitchens. This example is reputed in local folklore to be originally from Strata Florida and was preserved by the Powells of Nanteos who owned the site of the monastery in the later eighteenth century. By reputation, water or wine drunk from it could heal any disease, especially if the patient nibbled a little bit of the wood as well, hence its modern condition. It is currently on display in the National Library of Wales.

On the occasion of anniversaries and special feast days extra treats, known as pittances, such as eggs, fish or cheese might be allowed, and fine bread rather than the usual coarse loaves, but Cistercians were generally heedful of the strictures of St Bernard of Clairvaux against excessive consumption of food. Bernard was scornful of dishes that were elaborately cooked, citing the many ways in which eggs could be 'tortured': cooked soft or hard, scrambled, fried or roasted, or even stuffed. Like food, drink (wine or ale) was to be taken in moderation and not to interfere with the monks' performance of the divine office. Herbs were allowed but spices such as cumin 'which inflame lust' were frowned upon.

In the later Middle Ages, when dietary restrictions were softened, meat was allowed on special occasions and there was often a separate meat kitchen. As more exotic foods became more generally available, these too might occasionally appear in the Cistercian diet. This becomes clear not only in account books, such as that from Beaulieu Abbey (Hampshire) and Whalley Abbey (Lancashire) but also archaeological excavations, as at Øm Abbey (Denmark) which give evidence of the consumption of a variety of fish. We know that the monks of Strata Florida fished in the Teifi Pools in the mountains above the monastery, just as those of Meaux (Yorkshire) fished in Hornsea Mere.

Fig. 35:
Teifi Pools looking eastwards across the great open rough pastures of the Cambrian Mountains owned by Strata Florida (Aerial photograph by Toby Driver: RCAHMW AP DI2007_1679). These pools were famed for being well stocked with eels and trout. In the foreground are three sets of earthworks: the clearest (left of centre) are the remains of secular farms; (centre) a large structure probably for handling sheep; and less distinct, (right) a more complex set of buildings and a reservoir, probably the Cistercian *bercaria* (sheep-cote/farm).

Meals were announced by the ringing of a bell. Before entering, the monks washed their hands at the *lavatorium*, or basins that were located on either side of the refectory door. In the refectory the monks sat on benches at tables facing inwards. Overall responsibility for the meals lay with the refectorian and the cellarer whose task was the provisioning of the monastery. The kitchener and cellarer had already set the dishes on the table before the bell announcing dinner was rung. Before they were allowed to sit, the monks remained standing for a blessing and they were not to start eating until the prior, who sat on a raised platform at the southern end of the refectory, had sounded a handbell and uncovered his bread. The prior took precedence because the abbot dined in a separate chamber where he entertained guests. Above the raised platform there was often a cross, or, as at Cleeve Abbey, a large wall painting of the Crucifixion, with the Blessed Virgin Mary and St John on either side of the Cross. The large scale and architectural magnificence of many refectories reflect their importance as spaces of community life.

Fig. 36: Reconstruction painting of the refectory at Tintern (Terry Ball for Cadw) with the *pulpitum* for the reader of the day's text set high in the west wall (left-hand side).

Meals were taken in silence, and a reader, positioned in the pulpit or reading desk set above the level of the room, read from an appropriate book: the mind was nourished as well as the body. Two monks served their brethren on a weekly rota. *The Ecclesiastica officia* stated that in monasteries that did not have running water the helpers were to draw water for the monks to wash themselves, and for the table. One of them then set out the cooked portions, first for the novices, and then for the monks, while it was the responsibility of the other to collect the dishes at the end of the meal. On Saturdays they did the housekeeping: rinsing towels, scouring the basins, sweeping the latrines at the end of the dormitory, and carrying out the refuse. They warmed water for the *mandatum* (described above) and had a role in this ritual.

To the west was the kitchen, which was shared with the refectory of the *conversi* (lay brothers), itself located at the south end of the west range. To the east of the refectory was the warming room where a fire was permitted. The *Ecclesiastica officia* laid down that on Christmas night two lay brothers were to prepare a fire in the warming room for the monks to warm themselves during the interval after Vigils. Here they could seek some refuge from the biting cold of winter. Apart from the need for warmth the other permitted reasons for entering the warming house were for the monks to grease their outer footwear and to recover from blood-letting (on which see below). Whatever the occasion for entering, monks were warned that they should not go barefoot.

Washing and Shaving

The monks washed before Lauds, and washed their hands before meals, and their feet at the weekly Maundy. Baths were rare, both because they were deemed to be a luxury and because they might be a source of too much pleasure. For this reason, within the monastery, they were generally only allowed to the sick in the infirmary. Cistercian monks shaved seven times a year: before Christmas, just before Lent, at Easter, Pentecost (Whitsuntide), the feast of St Mary Magdalene in July, the Nativity of the Blessed Virgin Mary (8 September) and the feast of All Saints (1 November). The weekly kitchen helpers brought warm water to the cloister and the monks shaved each other. Regulations stated that the shaving of the crown of the head to form a tonsure (which was symbolic of monastic status) should not leave too narrow a strip of hair: nothing was left to chance. That these activities took place in the cloister is significant. As well as being – as we have seen – symbolic of Paradise it was the space of very earthly communal activities.

Fig. 37:
A manuscript from Abbey Dore (Herefordshire), depicting a monk being given his tonsure (London, British Library, Cotton Cleopatra, C.XI, f. 27v.)

Clothing: the Cistercian Habit

With typical wisdom and adaptability, St Benedict laid down that the brothers of a monastery located in a cold district could have more clothing than those in warmer climes. Wherever they lived, monks were to be content with whatever was available locally and cheaply. Cistercian regulations were determined on a return to the spirit of the Rule, and set down that clothing was to be simple, with no furs or undergarments of wool and linen. Benedict made provision for monks who had to go outside the monastery on business to wear tunics and cowls that were slightly better than the ones they usually wore, and to take breeches from the clothes cupboard which, on their return, they washed and replaced. Walter Map, a twelfth-century satirist, accused the Cistercians of trying to go one better, and forego breeches altogether. He tells the story of a Cistercian monk who while out of the monastery one day fell, and as he tumbled, a breeze lifted his habit. This – according to Walter – elicited a remark from King Henry II who was present about the Cistercians' 'bare-bottomed piety'.

The Cistercians were known as the White Monks. Whereas the Benedictines (the Black Monks) wore a habit that was dyed black, the Cistercians opted for undyed wool, straight from the sheep (and probably greyish rather than white). Walter Daniel, the monk of Rievaulx who wrote the life of his abbot, Aelred, likened them to angels, and, on another occasions and less flatteringly, to seagulls.

Fig. 38:
A fifteenth-century manuscript depicting the arrival of St Bernard with his monks at Clairvaux in 1115. The characteristic white habit has a black/brown apron (*scapula*) at front and back, usually worn for work (see also fig. 29). British Library Yates Thompson MS 32, f. 9v.

Silence

A Cistercian monk wrote of the profound silence of the monastery, in the middle of the day as well as the deep of the night, where the only sounds were those of the monks singing the offices or at their work. There was little speaking, and necessary conversations (such as those relating to the business of the monastery) took place in the parlour in the east range, generally next to the chapter house. If communication was necessary, then a form of sign language was used, with a range of gestures for people, food, actions, and emotions such as anger and sadness. Monks were warned, however, that such signs were for necessary communication only – such as asking for bread to be passed to them or indicating a need to visit the latrines – not for the conducting of conversations. After Compline the monks processed to the dormitory in silence, and no-one was supposed to utter a sound until the night office.

There would, however, have been many different sounds in the monastery: the soft murmur of the monks' voices as they read during periods of *lectio divina*; the chanting; the ringing of bells, perhaps a large one for the major offices and a smaller for the minor ones; the sounding of gongs; and gentle conversation as the monk officials such as the infirmarian went about their duties. In the wider precinct, there would have been the noises associated with the workshops, and the neighing of horses as guests arrived. Within the cloister, however, silence concentrated the monastic mind and removed the temptation to indulge in gossip which might foment disharmony.

Fig. 39: The silence of the Cistercian monastery could be broken by the sounds of quite large-scale industrial production. At the beautiful World Heritage site of Fontenay Abbey in the Côte d'Or in Burgundy, there is a very large water-powered forge building still standing within 30 metres of the main abbey buildings (A on the plan). At Strata Florida, too, excavations have revealed a similar structure within the inner court. The rhythmic striking of the hammer and the sound of the bellows would have been intrusive.

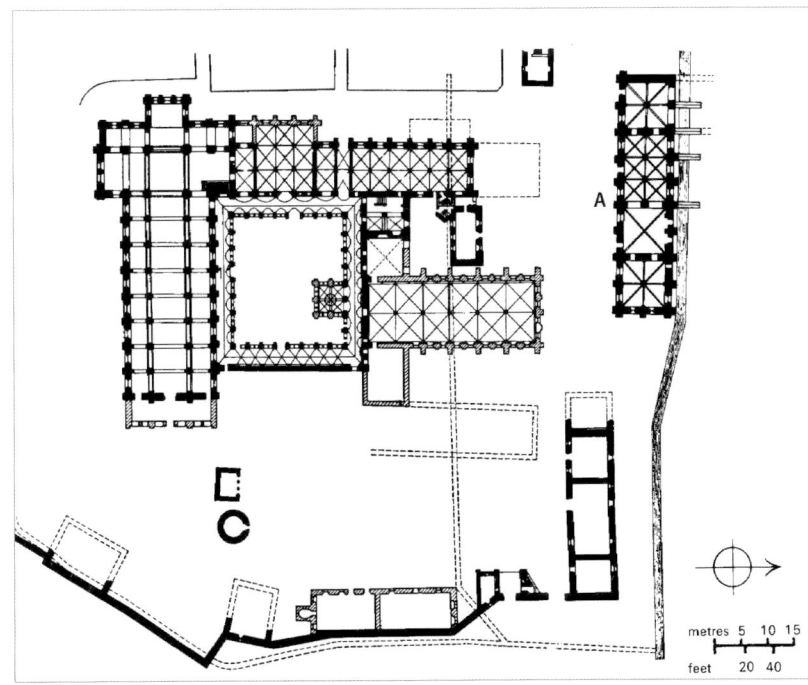

Becoming a Monk

Many men and women were drawn to the monastic life as a means to pursue their own road to salvation. Each one had a part to play, from the greatest to the least. Walter Daniel described his abbey as a place where all – great and small, young and old, learned and unlearned – were subject to the same law, and all were held as equals.

Postulant – Novice – Monk

Each Cistercian monk began his monastic journey in the same way as laid down in the Rule of St Benedict. As a postulant (one who asks or requests something) he arrived at the gatehouse seeking admission. This was not granted lightly, and after four or five days – if he was still there – he was led to the guest house, where he spent more days pondering his decision. If he clung to his ambition, he was led into the chapter house where he knelt before the lectern (reading desk). The abbot asked him what he sought, and he replied 'the mercy of God and yours'. He then formally entered the noviciate, a period of training that (in theory at least) lasted a whole year, during which he received instruction from the novice master. Not everyone would have survived this testing period: three times during his noviciate the Rule of St Benedict was read to the novice, and he was given the opportunity to change his mind.

Novices were not to be married men. If before he made his vows it was discovered that a man was married, he was expelled, and only allowed to rejoin if he could produce a letter from his bishop or a reliable witness to prove that his wife had taken a vow of chastity and had released him from the marriage.

Fig. 40: A thirteenth-century manuscript illustration of Bernard of Clairvaux writing, with two young pupils (Oxford, Bodleian Library, MS Laud Misc. 385 (Flores Bernardi, from St Augustine's Abbey, Canterbury), f. 41v).

Those who persisted proceeded to take their vows – obedience to the Rule and the abbot, conversion of life (that is, the adoption of the life of the monk), and stability (a promise to remain a member of the community for the rest of his life). If he was possessed of any property, he was expected to donate it to the monastery. He was then tonsured, that is, his hair was shorn in the shape of a crown, and the clippings burnt. His own clothes were taken off him and he received the monastic habit – a symbol of his change of life; in the words of St Paul, he was putting off the old man and taking on the new. His own clothes were kept in case he decided to quit the monastery – although it was not expected that he would do unless he listened to the 'persuasions of the devil'.

There would have been a variety of recruits, some of whom entered freely, from the ranks of the secular community and the clergy, and those who were perhaps less willing. There may have been family pressures – provision of a career for a younger son (or daughter, for there were houses for Cistercian women as well as men) – or economic pressures. Sometimes the demands of the monastic life proved too much. In his 'Life' of Aelred of Rievaulx, Walter Daniel, told the story of a novice who entered Rievaulx while Aelred was novice-master. He turned up at the gate of the abbey, and, having spent a few days in the guest house as prescribed by the Rule, was taken into the care of Aelred in the novice-house. Walter judged that the novice was not stable mentally – perhaps a harsh judgement – and described how he wavered and ran off before taking his vows. He wandered through the monastic enclosures and in and out into the woods which surrounded them. Circling round and round, he found himself back on the road to the monastery where he was received back by Aelred with tears of joy.

Subsequently, however, and having taken his monastic vows, he had further crises. He could not, he said, bear the demands of the monastic life: the length of Vigils, the manual labour, the bitterness of the food that he could not swallow, the rough clothing that bit into his flesh. It was – for the second time – the intervention of Aelred that persuaded him to stay and he ended his life as a Cistercian monk. The tale was told by Walter Daniel to emphasise Aelred's qualities: his patience, mercy, compassion, and concern for the weak – but his is a cautionary tale. The monastic life was not always an easy path. It involved more than commitment to the repetitive routine of its daily life. It demanded the renunciation of private possessions, absolute obedience to the abbot (even if a brother disagreed with him), the cutting of family ties and foregoing the possibilities of marriage and a family. For those who persisted in the Cistercian life the reward was salvation.

For Adults Only
The ritual for the reception of novices was laid down in the Rule of St Benedict, but the Cistercians made one significant change. Traditionally, there were two kinds of recruit to the monastic life. The first was the class of child oblates, children who were offered to the monastery by their families, there to be educated and to take vows at the appropriate time. The second group comprised the adult recruits who entered the monastic life in full knowledge of what this entailed. By the eleventh

century the practice of child oblation was falling out of favour, partly because of the issue of choice, and partly because the presence of young boys in the cloister was considered to be disruptive. St Bernard's own nephew, Robert, joined the Cistercians as an adult but was subsequently claimed by the famous monastery of Cluny (Sâone-et-Loir, France) and was persuaded that his home was with them because he has been oblated (offered) as a child. In writing to Robert to entreat him to return to the Cistercian fold, Bernard asked the rhetorical question of which had the greater force, a vow made by a grown man in full recognition of what he was doing, or a vow made on behalf of a child by his parents.

His fierce denunciations of child oblation chimed with the mood of the times. From henceforth, the Cistercians required that recruits to the monastic life should be at least sixteen years old, and this was later raised to eighteen.

Rising through the Ranks

Some monks remained in that station for their entire careers, spending their days in the routine activities of prayer, reading, and manual labour. Others, known as obedientiaries, rose to administrative or managerial positions. In larger abbeys these might take up much of their time around and even during the canonical hours.

The Top Job: the Abbot

At the head of the monastic community was the abbot. He was at one and the same time a manager, an authority figure, and father to his monks. It was not for nothing that the Rule of St Benedict reminded him that he would answer at the Last Judgement for how well (or not) he had executed his office. The Rule stipulated that the abbot was to be elected by the community, or the 'greater and wiser part' of it – a vagueness that might well lead to confusion and division. It was also laid down that there was no automatic pecking order: even the most junior monk was eligible. The Cistercians, organised as we have seen like a great family tree, widened the process for the selection of an abbot. The abbot was still to be elected by the community, but the election was to be overseen by the father abbot or his proxy (in one famous case from Yorkshire the proxy was himself elected as abbot). Moreover, Cistercians could look outside their own house for an abbot; the only person they could not choose was a non-Cistercian. So, heads of an abbey such as Whitland could be drawn from the house itself, or its daughter houses, or any Cistercian monastery. The first abbot would have come from the mother house with a founding community, Cynan of Strata Florida from Whitland, Philip of Valle Crucis from Strata Marcella, for instance. Firm evidence of the origins of abbots of Welsh houses is not always easy to find, and it is quite likely that they were promoted from within. In contrast, at the major Yorkshire houses of Fountains and Rievaulx we have evidence that in the first century of their existence their abbots had varied previous careers. In the twelfth century, Fountains drew its heads from Rievaulx, Vauclair (Aisne, France), Pipewell (Northamptonshire), Newminster (Northumberland), and Louth Park (Lincolnshire) – the last two were daughter houses of Fountains. Rievaulx was served by abbots drawn from its daughter houses of

Fig. 41:
Manuscript illustration of c. 1125 depicting Stephen Harding, one of the founding fathers of the Cistercian movement and author of its *Carta caritatis*. In the full image from which this is taken, Stephen is shown symbolically presenting his church to the Blessed Virgin Mary as Queen of Heaven and Earth (Dijon, Bibliothèque Municipale, MS 130, f. 104).

Dundrennan and Melrose in Scotland and Warden in Bedfordshire. These were houses of high status, however, and may not have been typical.

We know that the position of abbot could be one of prestige and importance. Ambition, rivalry among different factions within a house, or the desire of a patron to secure the promotion of a favoured candidate, could lead to disputed elections. At Strata Florida in the 1340s Llywelyn Fychan battled against Clement ap Rhysiart, a dispute that involved the General Chapter at Cîteaux, the papal curia, the bishop of Hereford, the Court of Arches (the court of appeal of the archbishop of Canterbury, the highest ecclesiastical authority in the land) in London, and Edward, prince of Wales (the Black Prince). This is a reminder that the office of abbot of a Cistercian monastery was not always just of local interest but could be of international significance.

Within his own abbey the abbot had important liturgical duties in choir, as noted above, taking the first place on the right-hand side towards the west, leading various antiphons (short musical pieces which may be used as a refrain, for instance, at the end of a psalm), and blessing the readers. He presided over the daily chapter and the collation before Compline. Because of the recognition of the importance of treating guests well, the abbot kept his own table where he entertained visitors. If there were no guests, he invited two monks to dine with him. In the early years of the Order, he slept in the monks' dormitory, but increasingly abbots built their own lodgings, which generally lay to the east of the east range, in the vicinity of the infirmary, as at Tintern, Fountains, and Byland.

Fig. 42: The detached abbot's lodgings at Netley Abbey, near Southampton, Hampshire.

At Valle Crucis, on the other hand, there is evidence that in the fourteenth and fifteenth centuries the monks' dormitory on the first floor of the east range was modified to create an apartment for the abbot, and several more for important guests. This may have been in the time of Abbot Dafydd ab Ieuan ab Iorwerth (1480–1503) who was well known for his generous hospitality.

Fig. 43:
The east range of Valle Crucis Abbey, with the monks' dormitory on the first floor. This was converted in the fifteenth century into the abbot's lodgings, with accommodation for guests.

A Cistercian abbot had a role to play within the Order through attendance at the Annual General Chapter and the annual visitation of any daughter houses that had been founded from his monastery. Unfortunately, the chapter records are not full enough to give us a detailed picture of who was at each General Chapter and who was not. We do know that in 1216 the Chapter excused the abbot of Aberconwy from attending because of illness, and in 1277 it was noted that the abbot of Tintern had not been present for some time, also because of illness. The latter was warned, however, that if he did not attend the following year he would be expected to resign.

Reluctance to go to the Chapter may in some cases be explained by the length of time it took an abbot away from his monastery and the potential dangers of travel. It could also be expensive, and in 1274 the abbot of Cymer borrowed £12 from Llywelyn ap Gruffudd, ruler of Gwynedd, to help cover his costs. Expenses could be incurred in other ways, and in 1220 Whitland acquired permission from the General Chapter to limit the hospitality he had to offer to English and Irish monks to fifteen days. The Irish abbots were doubtless on their way to the Chapter and enjoyed extended board and lodging at the Welsh house which was not far off the coastal route from Ireland.

The Chapter would delegate the investigation of certain matters to local abbots, and when this happened it is likely that the abbot received his commission in person – in other words, was present at the Chapter. In 1199 the Chapter, in considering the request of Madog ap Gruffudd of Powys Fadog to be allowed to establish a Cistercian monastery, ordered the abbot of Margam (south Wales) to take with him the abbots of Buildwas (Shropshire) and Whitland and engage in discussion with Madog as to what he was offering and the suitability of the site. The abbey he was to establish was Valle Crucis.

Annual visitation allowed a father abbot to make sure that all Cistercian regulations were being observed in relation to all aspects of life and administration, such as the maintenance of silence, the celebration of the liturgy, diet and clothing, the provision of hospitality. The *Forma visitationis* ('Form of visitation') of *c.* 1180 laid down the duties of the visiting abbot and the community. The former was to be vigilant and just, weighing carefully what he had learned, and not paying attention to gossip or backbiting. He was to correct with love and reverence and in a constructive manner. The community was expected to accept his criticisms with love and respect.

Other Officeholders

The prior was the second in command of the abbey – a responsibility that increased when abbots were absent for whatever reason. Certainly, the prior of Strata Florida would have been in charge for several weeks each year if the abbot fulfilled his expected duties of a yearly visit to the General Chapter at Cîteaux and the annual visitation of the daughter houses of Llantarnam and Aberconwy. In choir the prior stood opposite the abbot, at the first place (towards the west) on the left-hand side. It was his task to sound the gong to summon the monks to their work and to preside over meals.

The cellarer looked after the provisions of the monastery, making sure that everything that was necessary for life and worship was in adequate supply. Perhaps because he was in charge of provisions, the Rule of St Benedict stated that the cellarer should not only be prudent and mature but also 'not a great eater'. He helped to prepare food in the kitchen and oversaw it being dished out into individual bowls. At both dinner and supper, he did a tour of inspection of the refectory to check that nothing the monks needed was missing. He gathered up any leftovers, which were either kept to be served up again, or set aside to give to the poor. The need to communicate with those from outside the monastery – those bringing necessary goods and services – meant that the cellarer often had an office in the west range, as can be seen at Tintern Abbey in south Wales and Fountains Abbey in Yorkshire.

Fig. 44:
Above: the west range of Fountains Abbey claustral complex with the church to the left (north). The lay brothers' dormitory was on the first floor with access via external day stairs to be seen to right of centre; the cellarer's office was on the ground floor beneath the stairs. Below: the interior of the vaulted undercroft of the west range, which was the great storehouse of the abbey run by the cellarer.

The sacrist, or sacristan, looked after everything that was needed for the church and church services: candles, oil, liturgical vessels for mass, and vestments. These might be kept in a small room, or vestry, next to the church in the east range, where they would be easily accessible. Still within the church, the precentor (cantor) made sure that the liturgical books were in good condition. He led the chant during the church services and took care that all the monks kept alert and performed the offices well.

In addition to the cellarer two other officials were the interface between the monastery and the outside world. The porter, or gatekeeper, was, according to the Rule of St Benedict, to be a wise and elderly man, who knew how to take and receive a message, and who, located in a liminal space, would not be tempted to return to the outside world. Good examples of a two-storeyed gatehouse which was the porter's domain can be seen at Cleeve (Somerset), Stoneleigh (Warwickshire) and Kingswood (Gloucestershire).

Fig. 45:
Reconstruction painting of the excavated gatehouse at Strata Florida in its later medieval form, a two-storey structure with, perhaps, a chapel on the first floor. The building to the right may have housed the abbey treasury (a large number of coins were recovered here during excavation), and perhaps the prison, for which there is documentary evidence.

Once the porter had welcomed guests, he would hand them over to the guest-master, who – as his name suggests – was responsible in all matters for the guest houses. More will be said of guests below.

The Sick and the Dying

Following the Rule of St Benedict, provision was made for sick and elderly monks. It was recognized that age and infirmity may mean that they would not be able to fulfil all their monastic obligations, and allowances were to be made.

The Infirmary

Fig. 46:
Aerial view of Fountains Abbey from the west. The ruins of the infirmary block can be seen to the east of the main buildings, next to the River Skell.

A special room and attendant (later known as the infirmary and infirmarian) were provided. If it was felt that meat would be beneficial for the sick to keep up their strength, they were allowed to partake, and baths were permitted more frequently than for other members of the community. The work assigned to them was to be light and not tax them. They might be dispensed from attending all the offices in church and allowed to say the night office in the infirmary. If they felt fit enough, they could go to church where they would occupy the retrochoir, the space to the west of the pulpitum (screen) that marked the back of the monks' choir. Those who would find kneeling burdensome were allowed to sit.

When a monk presented himself to the infirmarian, the latter collected his bedclothes and his jug from the dormitory and at that point was allowed to speak to him and ascertain his needs. The infirmarian would need to know all the regulations about when (or if) a sick monk would still be expected to attend services and what extra food he would be allowed. He brought books from the church for those who were not fit to go to the offices and returned them afterwards. He made sure that silence was observed at the stated times and supervised the meals that would have been prepared in the infirmary kitchen. He would gather herbs from the infirmary garden for healing, and he was also responsible for regular blood-letting (unless there was someone to whom he could delegate this task).

Fig. 47:
A cutaway reconstruction painting by Terry Ball of the Infirmary Hall at Tintern Abbey as it may have appeared in the late thirteenth century.

Blood-letting was thought to be beneficial for health. Cistercian monks were bled four times a year. Certain times and occasions were avoided, and the *Ecclesiastica officia* suggested that appropriate times were February, April, and September, with a fourth bleeding around the feast of St John the Baptist (24 June). In preparation a fire was lit in the warming room (generally to the east of the refectory) and there the monks were bled one by one in groups. Afterwards, during the periods in which they should have been reading or working they were allowed to go into the dormitory and rest on their beds. They were permitted to sit in choir and given extra food to regain their strength.

Monks were only human, and the infirmarian had to keep an eye open for brothers who might feign illness to escape the rigorous routine and for a short while enjoy the comparatively relaxed atmosphere of the infirmary. St Bernard warned of those monks who – in order to give credence to their claims of weakness – carried a walking stick.

Death

There was a ritual around the dying and death of a monk which allowed members of the community to be a reassuring presence during the final hours and moments of one of their number. All the monks were present when he received the last rites of unction (anointing with oil), confession, and absolution, before leaving him in the care of the infirmarian who, as death approached, began preparations for his passing and burial. The dying monk was laid on a mattress sack under which ashes were spread in the shape of a cross. In the cloister a wooden gong was beaten rapidly, and the church bell was rung four times. As soon as they were able, his brothers made their way into his presence. As they gathered around, they said the litany (a form of prayer invoking the aid of the saints), and – if he was still alive – the seven penitential psalms. At the point of death they withdrew again.

When the brother had passed, more prayers were said, and the body taken away to be washed. The brothers gathered in the same order as they sat in choir and yet more prayers were said, while the body was brought in and sprinkled with holy water and censed. The monks then escorted the body, in procession into the church, where it was placed in the choir. Although some of the routine offices or services would have to be maintained, the abbot made sure that the body was never left alone. The *Ecclesiastica officia* gives no reason for this detail, but it was probably to ensure the maintenance of continuous prayers for the soul of the departed in the presence of his body.

Set times were allowed for funeral masses and the burial, depending on the time of the year, and detailed rituals were followed. The monastic burial ground or cemetery often lay to the north of the church, but in the case of Strata Florida it was located in the angle between the south transept and the presbytery, at the east end of the church.

Fig. 48: Recumbent slabs, some also with carved headstones using Celtic art motifs, found in the monastic burial ground at Strata Florida. These appear to have been covering important burials, transferred from the earlier site of the abbey at Henfynachlog. These probably include the grave of Cadell, brother of Strata Florida's great patron, the Lord Rhys of Deheubarth.

Abbots were often buried in the chapter house, where they remained as figures of authority, role models for their successors, and part of the communal memory. In the later Middle Ages, there seems to have been a move towards abbatial burial in the church. This was not unique to the Cistercians, and indeed the Benedictines appear to have started this trend rather earlier than the White Monks. There may have been more than one reason for this change in practice. The chapter house may have been getting full and lacked sufficient space for more interments, but this is unlikely to have been the only explanation. Burial within the church may have found favour because this was where there was a constant repetition of liturgy and prayers for the deceased. Additionally, by the later Middle Ages the church was probably accessed more by lay people and abbatial tombs would have been more visible there than in the chapter house.

'Bearded Lay Brothers': the *Conversi*

Within the Cistercian world the Latin word *conversus* took on a new meaning. It originally denoted an adult recruit to the monastic life, but under the White Monks it came to mean one who entered the monastery not as a monk but as a lay brother, a worker, in particular one who had a function in exploiting the monastic estate. In order to sustain themselves in their life of prayer and worship, the monks needed lands that would yield produce, and those lands needed farming and oversight. With limited time available for manual labour, and a reluctance for monks to leave the cloister, the Cistercians found a solution: the lay brothers. Unlike traditional monasteries that relied on the labour services of peasants and the use of servants, the Cistercians incorporated their workers into the world of their monastery and held out the opportunity of participation in the monastic life to others. They were not the first to recruit lay brothers: this innovation seems to belong to another new monastic order of the eleventh century, that of Vallombrosa. The Cistercians, however, were the first to use to the full the possibilities offered by this new class within the monastery.

The lay brothers took vows similar to those of monks: they committed themselves to the single life, and to spending the rest of their days in the service of the monastery. Moreover, a *conversus* was not allowed to change his vocation and become a monk. He participated in some liturgical duties, but there were only three prayers he had to learn by heart – the Lord's Prayer, the Creed (statement of Christian belief), and *Miserere mei, Deus* ('Be merciful to me, oh God', Psalm 51), but his main task was work. He was distinguished from the monk by being bearded (and not tonsured) and he did not wear a habit. His clothes consisted of coarse skins, a tunic, footwear (sandals or shoes), and a hood covering only his shoulders and chest. Among them, only those who served as blacksmiths were allowed to wear a smock, and it was to be black.

Some lay brothers were drawn from the noble classes, but these became the exception – indeed in 1188 the General Chapter ordered that any nobleman who wanted to enter a Cistercian house was to become a monk, not a lay brother. Although there is

Fig. 49:
Thirteenth-century doodle of a lay-brother: British Library MS Additional 48978, f. 41v

evidence that the ban on noble *conversi* was not always effective, most would have come from the peasant class, sometimes from the estates which were granted to the Cistercian abbeys, but becoming a lay brother was not a bad lifestyle choice: Cistercian abbeys and granges (centres of agriculture, production, and industry) offered a secure environment in which to work, and a chance of salvation. In times of population growth and pressure on land (such as the twelfth century) it could be an even more attractive option.

The *conversi* were not present at all the canonical hours, but for those services at which they were required they were accommodated in the nave. A screen topped by a rood (crucifixion), stood between them and the retrochoir (see above). At Rievaulx the *conversi* were said on feast days to have been packed in like bees in a hive. When the lay brothers were out working in the fields or the workshops they recited – at the appropriate hour – the few prayers they were expected to know by heart. On feast days they were to attend all the services and keep silence.

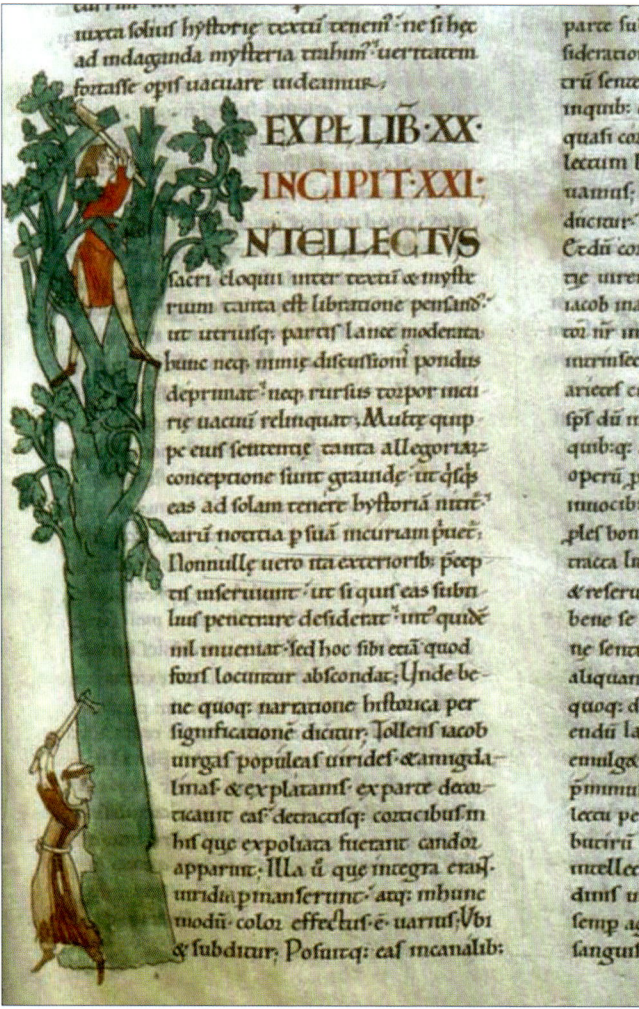

Fig. 50:
Monk and another figure (possibly a lay worker, *conversus*, or novice) felling and pollarding a tree. Dijon, Bibliothèque Municipale MS 173, f. 41r.

They did all sorts of work, and some of their tasks are outlined in the *Usus conversorum* ('Usages of the Lay Brothers') the earliest version of which appears to have been drawn up in the first twenty years or so of the Order's existence. Some worked on the abbey lands, managing the estates, tending animals, shearing sheep, and packing wool. Others were engaged in industrial activities, as blacksmiths and tanners, cobblers, weavers, and millers. They might conduct the business affairs of the monastery, allowing the monks to concentrate on their liturgical obligations and not have to travel to the markets and urban centres from which their wool was exported. At Strata Florida they may have supervised the fish traps at Aberarth, or the dispatch of the wool which the monks exported to Flanders by the early thirteenth century.

Fig. 51:
Left: aerial view of the fish traps at Aberarth, a former Strata Florida property, with the enclosed area, between the high and low tide levels, picked out in yellow (Toby Driver, RCAHMW). Right: the surviving structure of the fish trap seen at low tide.

Some of the lay brothers would have spent much of their time on the abbey granges and adjacent demesne centres, returning to the abbey only at major feasts. Within the cloister the lay brothers occupied their own space. They slept in the west range, paralleling the monks' dormitory in the east, and their refectory was located at the south end of the west range, where they shared a kitchen with the monks. Like monks they were to work in silence, and also refrain from talking in their dormitory and refectory.

The relationship between monks and lay brothers was intended to be one of equality – 'equal in life and in death' – but gradually there came to be a separation, with *conversi* treated as inferior. By the late twelfth century an indication of resentment lies in a number of revolts by lay brothers in several areas including Wales. In 1190 the General Chapter heard complaints about excessive beer-drinking by the *conversi* of Margam Abbey, who appear to have taken advantage of being away from the abbey on its granges to over-indulge. In 1195 the *conversi* of Abbey Cwm-hir stole the abbot's horses when he tried to stop them drinking. They were ordered to go to Clairvaux – on foot! – to do penance, the sentence being conveyed by the abbot of Strata Florida. We do not know if they made it, or even tried. Similarly, we do not know the nature of the 'excesses' among the lay brothers of Strata Florida that the abbot of the mother house of Whitland was ordered to investigate in 1196. Another indication of the growing separation is the presence in some monasteries of a lane, or passage, between the west range and the back of the cloister walk. Although its function has been debated, one effect was a more formal separation between the two groups. Good examples can be seen at Byland in Yorkshire and Neath in south Wales.

The relative size of the populations of monks and lay brothers is not often recorded and there must have been a great deal of variation over time and place. At Rievaulx in the late 1160s there were three times as many *conversi* as monks, but such mentions are only snapshots. Within four years of the foundation of Strata Florida it was recorded that there were thirty monks and forty *conversi*. At some houses the population of lay brothers would have been quite small, and their roles on granges may have been less agricultural and more managerial, with dependence on hired labour and the rents of tenants. Certainly, the coming of the Black Death of 1348 and 1349 brought fundamental change to a class apparently already on the wane. We do not know the rate of mortality in the Welsh abbeys, but at Meaux in Yorkshire not a single *conversus* survived the plague. Many abbeys found that those who did survive fared better under lay employers and had to rethink their economies.

Discussion of the *conversi* demonstrates that the monastic life changed and developed in response to external factors: economic, social, and cultural. It is important to remember, therefore, that they were a crucial element in the growth and success of the Cistercian Order. They held responsible positions within the monastic hierarchy and were important interfaces with the world beyond the cloister. Cistercian exemplary tales praise the devotion and spirituality of good *conversi* as they do of good monks, and equally hold up the faults of those who fell short. *Conversi* accompanied abbots on the long and often dangerous roads to Cîteaux, and abbots were not afraid to regard *conversi* as counsellors and advisors. It was on the advice of a lay brother of Fountains named Sinnulph that a knight named Ralph Haget became a monk, later rising to the position of abbot. Abbot William of Villers (Belgium) consulted Arnulf the waggoneer and when Arnulf distributed alms to the abbey's clients, he offered spiritual comfort as well as food.

'Guests who are Never Lacking in a Monastery'

The Cistercians, in following the Rule of St Benedict, took very seriously their obligation to provide hospitality – indeed chapter 53 of the Rule (from which this quotation is drawn) reminded them that they were to see Christ himself in every guest or stranger who arrived at the gate. Monasteries were an obvious place for the medieval traveller to seek hospitality, and some abbeys, particularly those with important patrons or those located on major routes (such as the Benedictine abbey of St Albans, which was situated a day's ride from London on the Great North Road) would have been visited more often than others.

We may imagine all sorts of visitors to Strata Florida: bishops, abbots, members of the lay elite, merchants on the road – some of them perhaps at Strata Florida to negotiate the purchase of wool – pilgrims, and wanderers.

Fig. 52: Part of a lead ampulla (a small flask containing holy water) carried by a pilgrim. This was found at Strata Florida in the gatehouse excavations. The front represents a cockle shell, originally the symbol of Santiago of Compostella but by the later Middle Ages a general badge of pilgrimage, and the back (here a drawing) may be some, unidentifiable, heraldic shield.

The Cistercian regulations provided for all of them. Some we can name. In 1188 Archbishop Baldwin of Canterbury and Gerald of Wales, archdeacon of Brecon and would-be bishop of St Davids (indeed, would-be archbishop), stayed at the abbey in 1188 as they journeyed through Wales preaching the Third Crusade. In 1238 Llywelyn ab Iorwerth of Gwynedd, doubtless accompanied by his younger son Dafydd ap Llywelyn, and the elite of Welsh political society gathered to hear the Welsh rulers agree to support Llywelyn's plan to be succeeded on his death by Dafydd alone. This was a challenge to Welsh custom which supposed the partition of territories among however many sons a man had, and it was wise for Llywelyn to arrange this great political set piece, even if after his death his plan imploded.

From the fourteenth century until the end of the life of the monasteries, Welsh bards were regularly entertained at Cistercian houses and praised the generous hospitality of the abbots. The fourteenth-century poet Dafydd ap Gwilym is reputed to be buried at Strata Florida. In the 1430s Guto'r Glyn sang the praises of Abbot Rhys, and later in the fifteenth century Dafydd Nanmor celebrated the restoration of the abbey church carried out by Abbot Morgan.

Fig. 53:
The death, in 1240, of Llywelyn ab Iorwerth, prince of Gwynedd, who was a great supporter of Strata Florida, as depicted in the chronicles of Matthew Paris, c. 1259. He is attended by his two sons, Gruffudd and Dafydd. Cambridge, Corpus Christi College, MS 16 (Matthew Paris, *Chronica Majora*), f. 132r

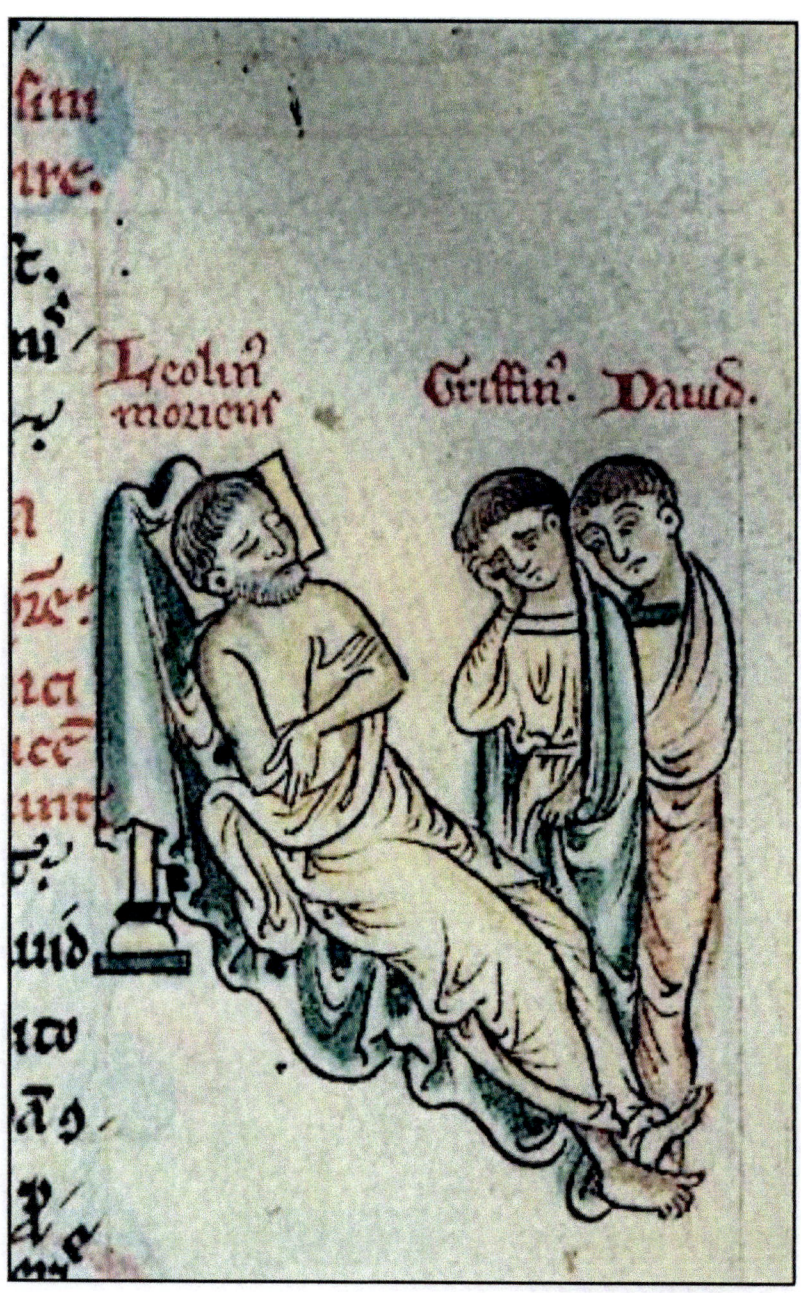

Like so much else of Cistercian life, the reception of guests was heavily regulated, however great or lowly they might be. The porter greeted newcomers with ritual words and invited them inside. As we have seen, the Rule stated that the porter was to be an old monk who could be trusted to give and receive messages and who would be less likely to be enticed away from his post by contact with the outside world. According to the Cistercian rules, the porter was not to admit women into the monastery – but there was often pressure from the local elite for him to do just that. Having greeted the guest, the porter would ask him to wait in the gatehouse and then would seek out the abbot (or the prior if the abbot was absent), to inform him of the visitor's arrival. The abbot (or prior) then indicated to one of the monks designated to welcome guests to make his way to the guest house to do so. The monk bowed before new arrivals, sprinkled them with holy water, and led them into the church to pray. After the visitors had finished their prayers, they were taken to the guest house where the guest-master attended to their needs.

Fig. 54:
Reconstruction drawing of the excavated fifteenth-century guesthouse at Kirkstall Abbey, Leeds, West Yorkshire.

There was sometimes more than one guest house. Fountains Abbey had a hall for visitors of lower rank and two for notables. There were evidently two halls at Strata Florida, for Gerald of Wales complained that he was accommodated in the one for the common guests, not the VIPs. At Scottish Melrose there were four. The guest houses often lay to the west of the claustral range, near to the gatehouse, as the more 'public' end of the precinct. It is here that we would normally find the *capella ante portas* or chapel before the gates, where visitors could attend services. At Merevale (Warwickshire) the gate chapel is now the parish church. Visiting abbots and high-ranking clergy would have stayed in the abbot's own lodging, which, conversely, usually lay to the east of the cloister, near to the infirmary. In the later Middle Ages retired abbots might build their own houses in this area – or have them constructed for them as a reward for their services or even as an incentive to retire.

Fig. 55:
The parish church at Hailes Abbey, Gloucestershire, which lies to the north of the abbey church and within the monastic precinct. It predates the foundation of the abbey but was used throughout the monastery's lifetime by pilgrims, guests, and the abbey servants. It boasts some fine medieval wall paintings.

Provision of food and drink for guests and their retinues, and stabling for their horses, might place a financial burden on monasteries, which would then seek permission to dispense with hospitality, despite the importance of this almost sacred duty. In 1258 Strata Florida was excused for three years.

The porter had other duties. He received from the cellarer any food left over from the refectory and distributed it to the poor who regularly gathered at the abbey gate. Gerald of Wales regarded Margam Abbey as the most generous of all Cistercian houses in Wales, offering as it did support to the needy of the vicinity as well as those passing through. In his account of his journey through Wales in 1188 he recorded that during a recent famine, when a large crowd of poor people gathered at the gate of the monastery, the monks sent a boat to Bristol to buy sufficient corn to allow them to feed those in need. The boat failed to return but the monks' compassion was rewarded when, the moment their own supplies ran out, a field was discovered near the monastery, all ready for reaping.

In 1194 the monks of Fountains Abbey responded in similar fashion by providing food, shelter, and both medical and spiritual care for the poor at their gates. Benefactors might grant land or rents specifically to finance such care, and one man specified that he wished to cover the monks' costs in providing head-coverings for those infected with head lice.

'Guests who Die in the Monastery'

In an effort to keep the world at bay the Cistercians would initially offer burial to a restricted number of lay people. These included members of their own *familiares* (paid workers and servants) and their kin, and those who, as guests, died within the monastery. In this respect they differed from the Benedictines. On the death of a guest, it fell to the prior and the guest house monk to make arrangements for burial. These were done quietly and sensitively, and the body was never left alone or without a light until the time came for burial. The deceased was taken into the church where the office of the dead, or a funeral mass, was performed. A bell was rung, and the community gathered around the body – but not if the burial took place at a time for work. In such a case the community was not obliged to attend. Guests would have been buried outside the church, probably in the vicinity of the chapel to the north of the abbey church: even in death, monks and laity were kept apart.

Fig. 56:
Somewhat unusually for a Cistercian abbey, the Strata Florida precinct incorporated a chapel to the north of the church provided at the cost of the abbot and convent. This was used for secular worship by the people of the locality. It provided burial and it still does today as can be seen on this vertical drone photograph. This unusual arrangement may have resulted from the abbey being, in 1184, located on top of a pre-Norman Christian site, perhaps itself of monastic form. A ninth-century carved stone was found during the nineteenth century, just to the east of the chapel and it is very likely that guests who died whilst visiting the Cistercian Strata Florida were buried in this cemetery.

The restriction of lay burial to guests was, however, a rule that was difficult to keep. Lay people valued burial within a monastery, particularly those who had founded the house, or their descendants who stood as patrons. Among the founders of Welsh Cistercian abbeys, Llywelyn ab Iorwerth was buried at Aberconwy, Madog ap Gruffudd at Valle Crucis, Owain Cyfeiliog at Strata Marcella. Hywel ab Ieuaf of Arwystli, an ally of the Lord Rhys, was buried at Strata Florida in 1185. The Lord Rhys himself chose burial at St David's, but his sons, Gruffudd ap Rhys (1201) and Hywel Sais (1204) were buried at Strata Florida. The precise location of their interment is not known. However, in the next generations, Rhys ap Gruffudd (d. 1222) and his brother Owain (d. 1235) were buried in the chapter house, where they were later joined by Maelgwn Fychan (d. 1257), his son Rhys ap Maelgwn (d. 1255), and Rhys's sister, Margaret, wife of Owain ap Maredudd. Despite the Cistercian reluctance to allow women inside their precincts, let alone bury them, the monks of Strata Florida also buried the widow of Gruffudd ap Rhys, Matilda de Braose, in 1210.

Fig. 57:
A large carved slab was found inside the chapter house of Strata Florida during Stephen Williams's excavations in the late 1880s. Beneath this stone, according to Williams's account, 'in a shallow grave about 2 feet deep, was found a mass of human bones and twelve or thirteen skulls. The latter had been carefully placed at the head of the grave, and were in fairly perfect condition.' This account suggests that the stone covered the re-interment of the remains of approximately the same number of members of the royal house of Deheubarth recorded, in the *Brut y Tywysogion*, as being buried in the chapter house of Strata Florida.

Sometimes, those who felt old age or death approach might choose to end their days in a Cistercian house. Those who enjoyed a particularly close association might be granted the privilege of dying clothed in the Cistercian habit. This was known as *'ad succurrendum'* ('as a means of salvation'), or deathbed conversion. This is what the compiler of the *Brut y Tywysogion* meant when he wrote that Cadell ap Gruffudd died at Strata Florida after assuming the monastic habit. The chronicler also notes that Cadell had died 'after a long infirmity' and he may have been cared for by the monks. The *Brut* similarly notes that Gruffudd ap Rhys died at Strata Florida in 1201, having assumed, or being clothed in, the Cistercian habit, as did his brother Hywel, who journeyed to the abbey having been stabbed by the men of his brother Maelgwn (1204).

'A Fish out of Water': Going Outside

Chaucer famously wrote that a monk who ventured outside his cloister was like a fish out of water. The Rule of St Benedict laid down that a monk who ventured abroad for whatever reason without the permission of his abbot was to be punished. That said, from time to time it might be necessary to leave the confines of the cloister. Abbots, as we have seen, were required by Cistercian regulations to be on the road at least twice a year. On other, less regular, occasions he might be out and about, delegated, perhaps, by the General Chapter to investigate disputes among abbeys or breaches of discipline. Abbots might also undertake diplomatic missions, as the abbots of Strata Florida and Aberconwy did in 1248 when bidden by Llywelyn ap Gruffudd of Gwynedd to negotiate with King Henry III of England for the return of the body of his father, Gruffudd, who had died in 1244 while trying to escape from the Tower of London.

A monk might be sent out on the business of the monastery, perhaps to deliver a letter to a bishop or a king, to negotiate trade agreements, or on a diplomatic or peace-seeking mission. On leaving and on returning he received a blessing, though this did not apply if he was able to return within the day. While absent – whether walking or on horseback – he was to say the office (though if riding he was to get off his horse first). A monk of Basingwerk in north Wales who – for reasons not recorded – stayed at Merevale (Warwickshire) was praised after his departure for his good conduct and 'religious conversion'. In the later Middle Ages monks were allowed to be away from the monastery to attend university.

Unusual Circumstances and Changing Fortunes

In many ways, life within a Cistercian monastery was unchanging. The liturgy carried on, day after day, though perhaps with increasing challenges once (as we know it did) the number of monks and particularly of lay brothers declined in the later Middle Ages. Recruitment fell, as men who might in earlier centuries have become monks sought other occupations. Additionally, as monastic resources diminished, a community might consciously decide to restrict recruitment. The Black Death hastened a fall in numbers among the lay brothers which in many cases led to a rethink and adaptation in economic practices.

Within the monastery time would still have been allocated around the offices for reading and manual labour. However, external pressures, often related to economic, political, and social environments, brought disruption. Abbeys in northern England suffered during the Scottish wars of the fourteenth century, while Welsh houses, often identified with the interests of their patrons (Anglo-Norman, English, or Welsh), might be subject to attack during times of heightened tension. In 1212 King John of England suspected Strata Florida of being in league with his enemies and threatened it with destruction. His men stopped short of physical damage, but the abbey was saddled with a large fine which they were still struggling to carry decades later. The impact on the economic fortunes of the house must have been significant.

The abbey – along with other Welsh Cistercian houses – suffered during Edward I's Welsh campaigns of the 1270s and 1280s, either through physical damage or the commandeering of goods and chattels. The monks were suspected of complicity in the rebellion of Madog ap Llywelyn in 1294/5 and ordered to cut down the trees and clear the paths around the abbey, presumably so that they could not harbour outlaws and suspect characters. Most famously, in 1401/2 the abbot appears to have been complicit in the rebellion of the would-be prince of Wales, Owain Glyn Dŵr, and in the two decades that followed, the English king's men stabled their horses in the church and stripped it of its plate – and we can only imagine trying to carry on with the offices in those circumstances. Poverty and demoralisation led to a threat that the convent would be dispersed, that is, its monks would temporarily be sent to other abbeys, and it was placed for two years under English administration. Forty years later the monks of Strata Florida still complained of the ruinous state of their monastery.

Accidents and natural disasters (fire and flood) also played their part in dislocating the monastic regime. In the mid-1280s (the date is given in different sources as both 1284 and 1286), a fire which apparently began in the belfry ripped through the church as far as the presbytery. Somehow, the abbots and monks of Strata Florida were to rise above the damage wrought by war, rebellion, and fire. A number of notable abbots of the fifteenth century began reconstruction and restoration, and bards marvelled at the glass windows, fine carvings, and the great belfry. Dafydd Nanmor remarked that the reputation of Abbot Morgan stretched as far as Cîteaux itself. For the monks this construction might have proved another distraction, as the shouts of men-at-arms and the neighing of horses were replaced by the sounds of a building site.

Another indication of change is the repurposing of various parts of monastic complexes. It was common, as the class of *conversi* disappeared, for the naves of monastic churches to be adapted to accommodate lay burials and altars, or even to fall into disuse. The reduction of the monastic population, as well as the social prominence of the abbot, seems to have been behind the remodelling of the monks' dormitory at Valle Crucis to make way for an abbot's chamber and guest lodgings (see above). The chapter house at Strata Florida was curtailed to accommodate fewer monks.

Fig. 58: Nineteenth-century excavations found large amounts of molten lead which had trickled down the walls and onto the floor surfaces of the abbey church. There were also extensive traces of fire on the masonry remains. It is uncertain as to which of the documented (or undocumented) destructive episodes these can be attributed.

The cloister became a more permeable space, with indications of guests or corrodians lodged there. A corrody was a kind of retirement plan made either by individuals or couples (known as corrodians), often purchased by them or offered by a monastic community as a reward for service. A monastery might undertake to supply the corrodian(s) with specified amounts of food, ale, or clothing, or a dwelling on monastic lands or in the precinct. In 1521 we have record of John Owain and his wife living in a chamber called 'The Candlehouse' which lay next to the church at Tintern and above the 'great door'. At Cleeve, under Abbot David Juyner (1435–87), the whole of the south range was rebuilt. The refectory on a north-south axis was also rebuilt so that it lay east-west and was (and still is) distinguished for its surviving magnificent timber roof with its angel carvings. It still occupied the upper floor, but the ground floor accommodated two apartments, each with a bedroom, a living room, and a latrine. These were designed for corrodians, who may have paid handsomely for their retirement package. At Hailes the infirmary was subdivided to provide accommodation for corrodians.

A court case involving Strata Florida which was heard by the king's commissioners at Shrewsbury in 1534, just a few years before the dissolution of the house, is illustrative of changing boundaries in the monastic precinct. Two witnesses differed in their accounts. Ieuan ab Hywel, a weaver, claimed that on the Saturday before midsummer day he had gone from the house of Thomas ap Gwilym at Strata Florida to the chamber of a monk named Richard Smith, within the abbey, to take him moulds for coining groats. Brother Richard came 'barelegged' to Ieuan's lodging (presumably the house of Thomas ap Gwilym), asking him to come and hear mass, and saying that everything was prepared for the counterfeiting. The attempt was not successful and Brother Richard – perhaps in a fit of pique – tossed the dud coins and moulds out of the window, where they were retrieved by a passing monk. He took them to the abbot, who came and arrested Brother Richard and Ieuan ab Hywel. Brother Richard told another tale, claiming that he had been drinking with Ieuan in the house of John ap Dyo, within the precinct of the monastery. After a few pots of ale, the monk settled the bill, and as he was making his way towards the church, Ieuan intercepted him and invited him to collaborate with him in the counterfeiting.

Fig. 59: Excavation of the abbey 'Great Gatehouse' in its early post-medieval form. The original roadway through the centre of the building was blocked with a new porch and door (foreground) when the structure was converted into a storehouse for the merchants who had taken over the wool production of Strata Florida for a fixed annual fee 'at farm'.

Well, they were found out and each blamed the other. What is interesting in the tale is not really who was to blame, but the indication of how the precinct had changed. As the monastic population had dwindled, it seems to have become less exclusive, with the individual lodgings of monks accessible to outsiders. Lay people might also become part of the communal worship, men such as Robert Blokeley who was appointed to keep the organs at Hailes in good repair, play them, and sing in the choir. The monks were adapting to new conditions.

The last century of monastic life has often been dismissed as a time of decline, a prelude to the 'inevitable' dissolution of the monasteries by Henry VIII between 1536 and 1540. Tales such as the alleged antics of Brother Richard Smith have fed into this narrative. It is therefore worth ending this account of monastic life within a Cistercian monastery with the positives. Cistercian monks were still aware of belonging to an international monastic order, as can be seen in the regular exchange of letters between English Cistercian abbots and Cîteaux, some of them relating to Welsh affairs. Abbeys like Cleeve, Hailes, and Forde were confidently investing in new building, and Abbot Marmaduke Huby of Fountains constructed his impressive tower and repaired the abbey granges. Dissolution came, however, and with it the end of a way of life that had persisted for a thousand years in different forms, and over four hundred years of a Cistercian presence. Nevertheless, the Cistercian vocation worldwide has endured, and in the twentieth century Cistercians returned to Wales, to Caldey Island which can be visited by boat from Tenby, and Holy Cross Abbey in Whitland, near to the site of the heart of the medieval Cistercian movement in Wales.

Fig. 60: A view of the buildings on Caldey Island, Pembrokeshire, created in the Arts and Crafts style by the architect John Coates Carter just before the First World War. Originally a re-foundation of monasticism on the island by Anglican Benedictines, by the time the building work was completed the community had converted to Rome. By 1928, however, the community was in debt and the island was sold to the Cistercian monks of the Abbey of Scourmont in Belgium in whose hands it remains today with a small community of Cistercian monks continuing the great traditions of the order.

Sources and Further Reading

Austin, David 2022, *Strata Florida: The History and Landscape of a Welsh Monastery*, Strata Florida: The Strata Florida Trust

Burton, Janet, and Julie Kerr 2011, *The Cistercians in the Middle Ages*, Woodbridge: Boydell

Burton, Janet, and Karen Stöber (eds) 2013, *Monastic Wales: New Approaches*, Cardiff: University of Wales Press

Burton, Janet, and Karen Stöber 2015, *Abbeys and Priories of Medieval Wales*, Cardiff: University of Wales Press

Kerr, Julie 2009, *Life in the Medieval Cloister*, London: Continuum

Robinson, David M. 2006, *The Cistercians in Wales: Architecture and Archaeology, 1130–1540*, London: Society of Antiquaries

Robinson, David M. and Colin Platt 2007, *Strata Florida [and] Talley Abbey*, 3rd edn (rev.), Cardiff: Cadw

Williams, David H. 2001, *The Welsh Cistercians*, Leominster: Gracewing

Acknowledgements

It is a pleasure to record my thanks to a number of people on whose help and advice I have relied. I am grateful to the series editors, Professor David Austin and Professor Dafydd Johnston, to the former especially for the invitation to write this book for the Strata Florida series and for his hard work with the illustrations. Dr Michael Carter of English Heritage read a draft and commented on it with his customary enthusiasm. My husband (as he always does) cast a kindly yet critical eye over the text. Over the years I have taught many courses on the Cistercians and generations of students have challenged me with the kind of questions I have sought to address here. To my PhD and MA students who gather (online) in a fortnightly 'Lampeter Medieval Researchers' group, and who, like Michael, read an early draft and offered suggestions: diolch yn fawr iawn.

David Austin and I have spent many long hours at Strata Florida over the years, walking the site deep in discussion, and I like to think that we have both benefited from our lively exchange of ideas. I have certainly learnt to see things in a different light. This is, I hope, an appropriate place to thank him for his years of friendship.

Illustrations:

We would like to acknowledge the following permissions and copyrights:

Creative Commons: Figs. 1, 3, 5, 17, 21, 26, 29, 39, 42, 46, 60

Royal Commission on the Ancient and Historical Monuments of Wales (RCAHMW): Figs 2, 35, 51 (left)

Cadw: Figs. 4, 14, 18, 24, 32, 36, 47

British Library: Fig. 6, 37, 38, 49

Bodleian Library, Oxford: Fig. 40

Dijon, Bibliothèque Municipale: Figs 41, 50

English Heritage: Fig. 12

The National Library of Wales: Fig. 31

Strata Florida Trust: Fig. 45, 59

Cambridge University Library: Fig. 9

Thames and Hudson: Fig. 28

Corpus Christi College, Cambridge: Fig. 53

Julian Ravest: Fig. 25, 56

Michael Carter: Fig. 55

David Austin: Figs 7, 8, 10, 11, 13, 15, 16, 19, 23, 27, 30, 34, 43, 44, 48, 52, 57, 58

Phil Cope: Fig. 20, 22

Lowri Goss, Fig. 51 (right)

Sheffield University 'Cistercians in Yorkshire' Project: Fig. 33

West Yorkshire Archaeology Service: Fig. 54